Have you been rejected by the one you love? You undoubtedly feel angry, depressed, bitter, sad or worthless. You may wonder if things will ever settle down again. Eventually they will, and you *can* recover your
—dignity
—self-esteem
—perspective
—balance
—security
—control
—sense of being lovable and valuable.

Bobbie Reed's prescription for your broken heart contains practical, tangible action steps. But no prescription can help unless the directions are followed. You *can* recover!

Prescription FOR A Broken Heart

Bobbie Reed

A Division of GL Publications
Ventura, CA U.S.A.

The foreign language publishing of all Regal books is under the direction of GLINT. GLINT provides financial and technical help for the adaptation, translation and publishing of books for millions of people worldwide. For information regarding translation contact: GLINT, P.O. Box 6688, Ventura, California 93006.

Published by Regal Books
A Division of GL Publications
Ventura, California 93006
Printed in U.S.A.

Library of Congress Cataloging in Publication Data
Reed, Bobbie.
    Prescription for a broken heart.
      1. Loss (Psychology) 2. Pastoral psychology.
I. Title. II. Title: Broken heart.
RC455.4.L67R44   1982   155.9'3   82-13274
ISBN 0-8307-0856-1

TABLE OF CONTENTS

Dedication

To my parents, Robert and Wilma Butler, with love, for teaching me to trust God and depend upon His Word not only in times of joy, but also in those of pain

To Zev, whose work in the field of relationships I admire, and whose friendship I appreciate.

BEYOND REJECTION

Imagine a pair of championship ice skaters executing a particularly intricate program with such close coordination that they almost seem to be one being. As they circle the rink, confidently performing the lifts and spins, sometimes apart, usually together, their moves are proof of long hours together perfecting the partnership. In the spirit of teamwork, at times one partner (or even both) may be off balance individually in order to counterbalance, or support, the other.

Consider what would happen if during such a moment one partner were to let go and walk away. The remaining partner would flail around trying to regain balance, stumble, fall and most likely sustain serious injuries.

That's pretty close to what happens when one person (dating partner, spouse, fiancé) decides to let go and walk away from a relationship. The rejected person is left to stumble and fall while trying to regain his/her personal balance. The resulting injuries are emotional, but the pain may also be physical. If you have been rejected, consider yourself to have sustained an emotional injury and take it easy for a while. You need a period of recuperation and recovery. Do only those things which are absolutely necessary. Skip the others. Don't make any unnecessary changes in your life for a while. Take care of yourself—there's only one you.

Recovery from a broken heart takes time. In fact, researchers claim that if you were to depend on time alone for healing, you can expect the recuperation to take roughly about half as long as the relationship lasted (i.e., three years for a six-year relationship; three months for a six-month relationship). However, Dr. Zev Wanderer (founder of the Center for Behavior Therapy in Beverly Hills, California and now in private practice in Malibu, California), after years of research and field-testing, has developed an approach which, if followed, can shorten the recovery time to twelve weeks regardless of the length of the relationship.

Many of the behavioral suggestions in, and much of the basic approach of this book are based on or borrowed from those outlined in his book.[1] What has been added to Dr. Wanderer's approach is the Christian perspective and biblical affirmations.

Dr. Paul Jongeward also contributed to this book by suggesting several ways of modifying the purely behavioral therapy approach to include the Christian perspective. His input as well as Dr. Wanderer's is greatly appreciated.

Because your response to the person you love is a learned behavior, it can be unlearned using the principles of behavior therapy. You cannot fall out of love using purely rational insights because emotional habits are so resistant to logic and reason that what you've learned on an emotional level cannot be changed at the cognitive level.

Therefore, the principles and techniques in this book can help you to deal with the emotional blow you have received and to stop the pain you are now experiencing. You will learn how to stop those thoughts of your beloved from controlling your mind, how to overcome your sense of helplessness and gain control, how to let go and move on.

This book will be most effective if you read (and reread) and follow the behavioral suggestions in one chapter each week, for twelve weeks. Note that each chapter includes an affirmation—based on Scripture—to build into your life. The Word of God has the power to heal our wounded spirits, transform our attitudes and overcome negative thoughts. (See Romans 12:2.) The affirmations should be read aloud each morning and evening and at least three times in between. Each week add the new affirmation from the next chapter so that by the end of the twelve weeks, you have twelve scripturally sound, positive attitudes you are using each day to overcome temptation, attacks from Satan, or your own weaknesses. Educational psychologists tell us that it takes three weeks of constant practice to substitute a good habit for a bad one. So it may take a couple of weeks for your new, positive attitudes to begin to show, but if you are faithful in using the affirmations you will soon develop a positive outlook on life.

Although this book can help you through the

rejection experience, it is not intended as a substitute for therapy. You will want to consult a trained, Christian counselor if you feel suicidal, totally out of control, or have a history of severe, emotional disturbance or substance abuse in times of stress.

During the first few weeks of your recovery your feelings will fluctuate. The road to recovery is not a straight, upward climb, but rather sometimes a case of three steps forward, and one step back.

Some days hope reigns, only to be supplanted by despair. Anger, depression, bitterness, longing, and feelings of worthlessness, like playful but undisciplined and noisy children, will chase each other through your mind mixing up your efforts to think logically or to make rational decisions.

But eventually things will settle down and you will recover. Recover what? Your

—dignity
—self-esteem
—perspective
—balance
—security
—control
—sense of being lovable and valuable.

The mourning process will not be pleasant, but it is essential for healing, and will vary from person to person. Some people will take longer to heal than others. But you will feel better soon, I promise!

Better yet, God promises: *Blessed are those who mourn, for they will be comforted* (Matthew 5:4, *NIV*).

Note
1. Zev Wanderer and Tracy Cabot, *Letting Go* (New York: G.P. Putnam's Sons, 1978).

CHAPTER ONE

BEING REJECTED

The person you love just walked out of your life with no intention of ever returning. You have been rejected. Rejection is always a shock. Even if the relationship had been deteriorating for a long time, and you had been afraid that a parting of the ways was inevitable, you are probably unable to actually believe that this time the relationship is truly over.

As you consider your life, you feel as if you have lost the only thing of any value—the love relationship with that special someone. "What else matters," you ask yourself, "if my beloved no longer loves me?" Somehow, all of the other things, activities and relationships which had meant so much to you (a career, your family, children, friends, hobbies, clubs, church activities) suddenly lose their significance. It seems that only being loved by the one you love can bring meaning back into your existence.

So you feel wounded, lost, hopeless, helpless,

defeated, unmotivated and, most of all, betrayed. It wasn't supposed to end like this!

Love—A Fantasy

Romantic love, according to Dr. Dwight H. Small, is like having a magic mirror. The reflection of oneself in the eyes of the beloved is exciting, wonderful and attractive. Because her partner finds her desirable, a woman feels desirable. Because his partner sees him as having unlimited potential, a man experiences a transforming vitality.

Most people "in love" temporarily lose touch with reality and begin to live a fantasy existence. As unbelievable as it may seem to them at first, the fairy tale of the magic of being in love has apparently come true. It's fantastic! Love is everything the books, movies, songwriters and poets claimed—and more! Eyes sparkle. Cheeks flush. Tender glances share so much. Life becomes an adventure for two.

And, since this much of the fairy tale turns out to be true, the happy couple reasons that *living happily ever after* must be their destiny.

Loss—A Tragedy

If being "in love" makes life a fairy-tale existence, then being rejected turns it into a melodramatic tragedy. Not only has a special person gone out of your life, but with him/her also went the sparkle, the adventure, the fantasy. You may even find it difficult at first to distinguish between the pain of losing the person and that of missing the fantasy.

You will probably experience extreme, and possibly frightening mood swings from hope to despair, from jealousy to indifference, from anger to longing. By the end of each day, having run the entire emotional gauntlet, you will feel battered, bruised and exhausted.

Uppermost in your mind is the question of how to get your loved one to return and resume the relationship. You don't want another love, not even a better one! If you genuinely believed that there were no hope for a reconciliation, you might even wonder why you should continue living.

You must. Because you will feel better soon. Because you can recover from a broken heart. Because you are stronger than you think you are. Because even if you don't feel loved right now, God loves you and cares about your pain. *Cast all your anxieties on him, for he cares about you* (1 Peter 5:7, *RSV*). And in Psalm 56:8 David says that God catches our tears in His bottle and records them in His book.

Withdrawal Symptoms

Only the romantic partner can keep the fantasy alive. So romantic love is addictive by nature, causing partners to form dependencies which require contact and interaction with one another.

When one partner becomes disillusioned with the relationship and walks away, the abandoned partner, now deprived of romance, experiences withdrawal symptoms. And, just like other addicts cut off from their supply and suffering the pain of withdrawal, the rejected person has an almost irresistible urge to contact the beloved for a "love fix." At first there is often genuine physical pain as the body responds to the emotional trauma. Chest pains, stomach cramps, ulcer flare-ups, muscle spasms in the back or neck and headaches are common to the rejection experience.

Your own withdrawal response may include such typical behaviors as: not being able to concentrate on any task, thinking that you are going insane, feeling that you are a total failure, insomnia, a change in eating or sleeping habits, planning elaborate ways to win your beloved back, crying, neglecting yourself, your children or your job or having numerous exaggerated fears.

Evaluate the degree of your addiction by using the following checklist developed by Dr. Zev Wanderer and Tracy Cabot.[1] If you do *most* of the behaviors listed virtually *every day*, you are probably suffering an acute case of withdrawal and may need to seek help from a qualified, Christian counselor.

It is important to note that all of the behaviors listed are normal responses to the rejection experience. You are not going crazy if you suddenly find yourself behaving in these ways during the first few weeks after being abandoned.

Check yourself.

Obsessive Behaviors

1. Not being able to concentrate on any task

2. Watching the telephone and waiting for it to ring, expecting that your beloved will call

3. Listening to sad music, feeling the words were written just for you

4. Imagining that you see your beloved everywhere you go

5. Spending long hours holding imaginary conversations with your beloved during which he/she returns to your loving arms

6. Giving up responsibility for your life; thinking that whatever happens, happens

7. Thinking about going insane, being committed to an institution and being taken care of

8. Thinking of ways to make the beloved suffer for rejecting you

9. Remembering all of the nice things your beloved said and wondering if they were all lies

10. Feeling overwhelmingly guilty about your failures in the relationship

11. Thinking that you have lost the "one and only" for you

12. Not being able to make any decisions and feeling insecure about all of your opinions

13. Experiencing constant pain

14. Wishing desperately that you could start over

15. Considering killing yourself so your beloved would be sorry for rejecting you.

Compulsive Behaviors

1. Pursuing strange cars or people thinking they are your beloved

2. Interrogating mutual friends about your beloved

3. Talking to anyone who will listen about how you've just been rejected, hoping for comfort or advice

4. Begging God to make your beloved come back to you

5. Starting to eat a lot of junk foods or to drink alcoholic beverages

6. Starting to smoke

7. Having only one goal in your life—to win back your beloved

8. Driving by your beloved's house, office or

favorite places, hoping to see him/her

9. Shopping for gifts to give your beloved to celebrate your making up

10. Keeping all of your beloved's favorite foods in the house in case he/she comes over

11. Planning for the time when your beloved will return

12. Buying clothes which will entice your beloved to return

13. Telephoning your beloved again and again

14. Reading lovelorn columns and magazine articles searching for advice on how to win your beloved back

15. Buying cards to send to your beloved which will tell just how you feel without his/her love.

Depressive Behaviors

1. Sleeping all of the time

2. Not being able to work effectively

3. Thinking all of the time about going home to bed

4. Not being interested in going out or doing anything

5. Not taking care of yourself or your house

6. Neglecting your pets, plants, job, children

7. Letting bills pile up unpaid (even though you have the money to pay them)

8. Crying excessively

9. Rejecting offers of friendship or love

10. Feeling helpless and hopeless and as if you were a total failure

11. Feeling that nothing is of any use or value, so you give away possessions, and discontinue participation in your various clubs, organizations or church activities

12. Not being able to cope with even insignifi-

cant problems, such as jars which won't open, traffic jams or burnt beans

13. Feeling suddenly fat, skinny, unattractive, unloved or unappreciated

14. Thinking about, planning or attempting to kill yourself

15. Taking foolhardy risks because you feel that the worst has already happened to you.

Phobic Behaviors

1. Feeling that the world is closing in on you and you can't take it

2. Feeling panic at the thought of meeting new people

3. Not being able to stand ever being alone

4. Wanting to leave all of the lights on and the doors open in the house

5. Being afraid of growing old and being alone

6. Being afraid that you are losing your mind

7. Thinking you are losing your looks

8. Avoiding places where you and your beloved went together

9. Being afraid of not being able to support yourself

10. Wanting to run away

11. Wanting to sell everything you own and move to another city

12. Being afraid that you have ruined your life forever

13. Being afraid that no one will ever love you again

14. Being afraid that you might kill yourself

15. Being afraid of what your friends and family will say about anything you do or say.

Psychosomatic Behaviors
1. Having frequent, acute attacks of heart-burn, nausea, or diarrhea
2. Feeling nauseated at the sight of food
3. Having chest pains
4. Losing your desire for sex
5. Having a rapid heartbeat
6. Having your blood pressure go up
7. Developing an ulcer
8. Having pimples, psoriasis or unexplained rashes
9. Having an onslaught of physical illnesses such as flu or colds
10. Starting to bite your nails
11. Developing back or neck pains or muscle spasms
12. Waking up frequently in the middle of the night
13. Having allergy or bronchial attacks
14. Getting indigestion whenever you eat
15. Having frequent, severe headaches.

Hysterical Behaviors
1. Getting irritable at the slightest provocation
2. Letting little things cause you to panic
3. Forgetting important things you have to do
4. Losing your temper frequently
5. Not being able to stand the silence (having to have the radio, stereo or television on all of the time)
6. Not being able to stand noise (such as construction, freeway traffic, airplanes, music)
7. Always feeling cold
8. Wanting to smash or break things
9. Feeling that your emotions are all out of control

10. Driving around aimlessly and sometimes getting lost
11. Missing or canceling appointments
12. Fantasizing about killing your beloved
13. Becoming careless and having accidents
14. Becoming loud or bursting into frequent, uncontrollable laughter
15. Feeling that you would give anything, do anything, or promise anything, just to get your beloved to return.

Anxious Behaviors

1. Not being able to sleep well
2. Not being able to eat
3. Having accidents, hurting yourself and ruining things
4. Driving carelessly and getting tickets
5. Not being able to breathe deeply
6. Having tension headaches
7. Gritting your teeth
8. Grinding your jaw
9. Perspiring excessively
10. Having cold and clammy hands and feet
11. Having your face feel tense all of the time
12. Developing deep furrows in your forehead
13. Feeling nervous and touchy
14. Worrying constantly about everything
15. Overreacting to situations.

Breaking the Addiction

Now that you've recognized your newly adopted behaviors as basically withdrawal symptoms, your next step is to "kick the habit." Learning to live without the one you love probably sounds as impossible and undesirable as living without alcohol or drugs sounds to an alcoholic or drug addict.

But you can succeed.

Your immediate need is to stop this unbearable pain. The principles and action suggestions outlined in this book are proven behavioral techniques developed and field-tested by professionals working with thousands of people suffering from rejection. They do work. They will help you break the thought-addiction you have to that special someone, so that you can think clearly about your life and the choices you are making.

The first week will be the worst. And the next few weeks might be compared to a roller coaster ride—highs and lows, rushes and slowings, wanting to scream and feeling as if the bottom were dropping out from under—a sense of being out of control. But as you take the positive steps suggested, you will soon discover that the pain is subsiding, the wound is healing and life is getting brighter once again.

Is Anybody Listening?

Since you can't talk to your beloved, then you have probably discovered that talking about the one you love is the next best thing. A little of the pain seems to go away if you can at least share about the fantasy-like love you once had. So you have a compulsion to become incredibly garrulous, sharing with anyone and everyone you know or meet, all the details of your rejection experience.

Don't.

There are several reasons not to give in to the desire to communicate what's happening in your life just now:

First, doing so will continue to feed the addiction and prolong the withdrawal period.

Second, the advice you will receive will tend to be contradictory and confusing. Some people will say to forget your love. Others will cheerfully assert that you are better off without that person in your life. A few will weep with you; others will possibly gloat with "I tried to warn you that this would happen." You really don't need to hear all of that right now. So wait a while to start talking.

The third reason to keep your own counsel at this time is that it is too soon to be sure the relationship is truly over. There is always a possibility of a reconciliation, which would be a lot easier if you haven't gone around announcing the breakup and sharing all of the intimate details of your last bitter scene together.

This doesn't mean, however, that you have to hold all of your thoughts bottled up inside. God is listening. Tell Him everything you are thinking, feeling and wishing. Verbalize your hopes and fears. He is the greatest confidant and comforter. He understands. He cares.

You might find it helpful to read about Christ's own experiences with being rejected. David describes the physical pain and the sense of abandonment Christ was later to experience as He hung on the cross, deserted not only by the ones He loved, but also by God who turned His face away from the sight of Christ on the cross. (See Psalm 22:1-22; Matthew 27:46; Mark 14:32-41.)

As you read Psalm 22, compare how you are feeling to how Christ felt. Identify differences and similarities. Talk to God about the rejection experience and the difficulties you are having with coping.

You may also decide that talking with a counselor, your pastor or one close friend would be very helpful. No matter whom you do talk with, you will probably still have a compelling impulse to contact the love of your life. Gary used to call Valerie several times a day just to hear the voice he loved. (He didn't always say anything; sometimes he would hang up right after she said "hello.") Betty used to drive by her former boyfriend's house, or past his office building, hoping to catch a quick glance of him.

If contacting your beloved is what you genuinely want to do during the first week of rejection, then use the telephone and make the call. The outcome of contacting your love will probably be positive, regardless of what happens. If the person you love is kind, gentle and caring, your pain may be temporarily lessened. On the other hand, if that person is rude or hangs up the phone, part of the romantic fantasy starts to fade. It's easier to let go of a rude reality than a romantic fantasy.

If after talking to God, your pastor, a counselor, a close friend, and your beloved, you still feel a need to communicate your thoughts, try these suggestions.

1. *Write your thoughts.* Make lists. On one sheet of paper list everything you want to remember to tell your beloved the next time you talk. On another, list all of the things which went wrong between you. A third list might be everything you want to remember about the relationship. List your hopes and fears. Write until you have nothing left to say. It helps. Then put the first list by the telephone for easy reference, and put the other lists out of sight. Don't share with anyone else what you have written at this point.

2. *Visualize the person you love* sitting in a chair or on the corner of your sofa and verbalize everything you want to say to him/her, but cannot (or will not). Speak with feeling, just as if that person were actually there. Express your longing, your fears, your love, your hopes and desires. Talk until you have nothing new to say and grow tired of repeating yourself.

The Midnight Hours

Most people agree that the pain of rejection intensifies at nighttime. The house is somehow filled with your loved one's absence and sleep is elusive.

Be creative.

Don't sleep in that double bed you've shared with your spouse for the last ten years. Sleep on the sofa. Or in the guest room. Build a warm fire in the fireplace and "camp out" in front of it in a sleeping bag. Let your children sleep with you for a few nights. Invite a friend over to spend the night. Let the dog (or cat) sleep at the foot of your bed. Leave the lights on all night. Leave the stereo, radio or television on all night for the illusion of human contact.

If you think something might help you (and it won't harm you or others), then try it. You may discover a way to temporarily ease the pain.

Focus on Essentials

During this period of recovery from rejection, you may not be able to maintain your usual busy schedule of chores and commitments. So, give yourself permission to focus on the essentials only and don't expect yourself to function at your optimum capacity for a while. Try to rest. Get as much sleep as you can. Take naps if needed. Plan to go to bed early and sleep in. Take life slower; don't rush around as much. Rest your emotions for a few weeks. Don't let things get you all upset or super involved.

For the first couple of weeks, reduce house-cleaning to a minimum, eat simply, postpone commitments, and don't start new projects. Take time to incorporate the following affirmation into your life. Your spiritual life is an important essential you won't want to neglect.

Affirmation of Strength
Jesus gives me strength for this experience. Repeat this affirmation several times a day. It is based on the following Scriptures:

Deuteronomy 33:25—*As your days, so shall your strength be (RSV).*

Ephesians 3:16—*I pray that out of his glorious riches he may strengthen you with power through his Spirit in your inner being (NIV).*

Philippians 4:13—*I can do all things through Him who strengthens me (NASB).*

Note
1. Zev Wanderer and Tracy Cabot, *Letting Go* (New York: G.P. Putnam's Sons, 1978).

CHAPTER TWO

PATCHING IT UP

In spite of the pain you have suffered you probably still hope that there is a chance for you and your beloved to get back together again. Several times a day you mentally play out the touching reunion scene you hope to experience.

Roger's fantasy went something like this: He would be working in the garage and hear a car door slam shut in front of the house. Turning around slowly, he would see Wanda running across the lawn toward him, tears streaming down her face. He would drop his tools and rush to meet her at the door. Crying and clinging together, they would promise each other eternal love and togetherness.

Rachael's fantasy was different. She pictured Allan returning "on his hands and knees," begging to be forgiven for having caused her so much pain, and vowing to never hurt her again. She would then graciously (self-righteously?) forgive him.

In Melodie's dream of reconciliation, she would

continue to shower her beloved with kindness, gifts, cards and helpfulness (doing his laundry, cleaning his apartment) until he would realize how much she still loved him and wouldn't be able to resist her love. Then he would break off the new relationship he had developed and come back to Melodie, forever.

Whatever your own fantasy may be, it is basically an indication that you have not yet given up on the relationship. This may be a good sign. The problem with fantasies like Roger's, Rachael's and Melodie's is that they are still perpetuating the fairy-tale aspects of romantic love. Repairing a relationship requires more than a tearful reunion. The problems which caused the relationship to break up must be resolved if there is to be any future for it.

There May Be Hope

Sometimes relationships are stronger than ever before after a temporary separation and subsequent reconciliation. This is possible when:

1. *Both persons* want the reconciliation.

2. *Both persons* realize that what they almost lost was precious and valuable to them.

3. *Both persons* decide to direct some priority time and energy into making the relationship work.

4. *Both persons* agree to forgive the other for past wrongs and failures and present imperfections.

5. *Both persons* agree to accept professional counseling to resolve significant problems in the relationship.

6. *Both persons* put Christ in the center of

their lives and seek His will for their futures.

The first two words of each of the six conditions listed above are significant. Strong, healthy relationships are the result of joint efforts by *both persons* involved. Supposing only you want the reconciliation. Does this mean you shouldn't try? No. Only that your chances at success are very slim. Usually when only one person wants a reunion, and is willing to work at the relationship, then that person permanently assumes the *giver* role, which results in the other person becoming a *taker*. The *giver*, afraid to allow any opportunity for the *taker* to walk away again, will sacrifice anything for the sake of the relationship. The *giver's* personal preferences, ideas or needs are discounted and ignored, while the preferences, ideas and needs of the *taker* are given priority attention.

There are problems inherent in this approach to relationships:

1. *Givers* usually end up feeling used, unloved, and that they are not seen by the *takers* as persons of worth.

2. *Givers* may become resentful.

3. *Takers* may begin to develop a sense of guilt because of that role, and resolve the guilt by walking out of the relationship.

4. *Takers* may become bored with living with a "yes" person and break off the relationship.

In healthy relationships both persons learn to give and take; one-sided alliances are not really very strong. So, in attempting to effect a reunion, proceed cautiously and try to avoid pitfalls which might result in a one-sided relationship. And remember that there are several good reasons for attempting a reconciliation.

Why Try?

It might work! That's a terrific reason to try to get back together with the person you love.

Perhaps that person secretly wants to reconcile also but is too proud, ashamed or afraid to make the first move. Your taking the initiative makes it easier for the other person.

If it is a marriage which you are trying to save, you will want to know that you have tried everything to save a relationship which is ordained by God. And if you try now, later you won't suffer the guilt of "If only I had . . ."

Even if your efforts at reconciliation fail, they will keep you in touch with the reality of the situation. When you are alone thinking about your beloved, you are probably focusing only on your positive memories. Your concept of that person can easily become distorted until you no longer remember anything negative about the one you love. So, when you contact that special person and have to deal with the realities of his/her personality, your perceptions are tested and hopefully realigned.

"I couldn't wait to meet Ken and discuss our getting back together," she shares. "All I could think of was how wonderful it was going to be. I even hoped that after a long lunch he would decide not to go back to work, but to spend the rest of the day together. I was at the coffee shop half an hour early. Then Ken showed up. He was forty minutes late, had a buddy from work with him, and said he had to hurry back to the office because they were so busy. Wow! Did my bubble burst quickly! I had to realize that our reuniting was not the most important thing in the world to Ken, as it was to me. We met several times after that first day and tried to discuss our relationship, but he was never willing to set aside the time to really communicate!"

Proceed Prayerfully

Approach your reconciliation seriously rather than impulsively. Before you make that first call, spend a quiet evening with God. Read His Word. Ask the Holy Spirit to search your heart and reveal to you those areas where you need to grow and develop in order to be a better partner in a relationship. Write down those things which He brings to your mind. Make a sincere commitment that you will approach your partner in a Christlike, forgiving spirit rather than from a hurt, resentful or judgmental position.

Be careful not to mistake a feeling of expansive generosity—a "what's-done-is-done" attitude—toward your beloved for true forgiveness. Forgiveness is also not a desperate, bargaining "nothing-else-matters-if-you'll-come-back-to-me" position. Instead, true forgiveness comes from God who gives us the ability to say, "I have forgiven the past the way God, for Christ's sake, has forgiven me."

The generosity or bargaining approaches are emotional acts; genuine forgiveness is a rational commitment. Ask God to prepare the heart of the one you love so there will be a receptiveness to your attempts for reconciliation. Ask for guidance and wisdom as you plan how to approach your beloved.

Now is the time to contact that special person and arrange a face-to-face encounter to discuss the possibilities of your getting back together.

Starting Over

If that discussion is successful and you have agreed to at least attempt a reunion, terrific! Now the hard work begins. Obviously, there will have to be behavior changes on both sides. The old relationship didn't work. You are about to build a new relationship which salvages all of the good materials from the previous one, but which (hopefully) discards the bad.

One method of identifying which behaviors will make the new relationship a solid structure is for each person to write three lists:

1. Behaviors which enhanced our prior relationship

2. Behaviors which detracted from our old relationship

3. Behaviors which could strengthen our future relationship.

The first list, by highlighting the positives in the old relationship, affirms both partners. It might include such things as:

—*your cooking attractive meals*

—*our spending every Thursday night with the children*

—*your remembering my birthday and holidays*

—*your complimenting my appearance*

—*my listening when you share about work-related problems*

—*your keeping the house neat*

—*my doing yard work*

—*your support when I lost my job.*

The second list identifies actions (usually of the other person) which are irritating or hurtful. It is basically a list of grievances. (But remember that you have made a commitment to God that the past is forgiven, so list behaviors which may cause problems in the relationship in the future, and don't bring up one-time offenses from the past!) Things on the second list might include:

—*your spending so much time on the telephone with friends*

—*your bringing home work from the job every night*

—*your spending every leisure hour in front of the television*

—*your interrupting me when I'm telling jokes*

—*your hassling me the minute I walk in the door from work*

—*your being so jealous I can't talk to another woman/man*

—*your being late to everything*

—*your being critical of my work, friends, home, cooking.*

The third list tends to be those behaviors which the person wants substituted for those on the second list. For example:

—*your spending at least one hour alone with me each day*

—*your listening when I share with you, instead of reading the newspaper at the same time*

—*your waiting until after dinner to discuss problems you had during the day*

—*your being on time (or even early occasionally)*

—*your giving me at least one compliment a day.*

When you have both completed your lists, start

your discussion by concentrating on your first lists. This way you begin the discussion on a positive note as you share those things which made your relationship special to each of you.

Next select some of the important behaviors on the third list which you want to request of one another in order to improve your relationship. Try to pick those positive behaviors which will also begin to eliminate behaviors from the second list.

For example, you may ask your spouse to spend at least one hour alone with you each day (see sample list three) which could replace problem behaviors from the second list, such as

—spending so much time on the telephone with friends

—working so many hours at home

—watching excessive television.

Or, your spouse might ask you to wait until after dinner to discuss problems you had during the day (see list three) instead of hassling him/her the minute he/she walks in the door from work at night (see list two).

Keep the conversation positive, and don't let it deteriorate into a nonproductive argument. Agree on two or three behavior changes which each person will make. Set a time for the changes to begin. Decide how you will remind each other lovingly of your agreement whenever one of you "breaks the contract." Have prayer together, restating your commitment to this relationship.

Building your relationship into a strong and healthy union will require a daily commitment by both partners, but the results are well worth the efforts.

It's Really Over

Perhaps you gave it your all, but the other person just didn't seem to care and you are beginning to think that the relationship is really over. Trying to reconcile was still worth your time and energy because, in the process, you've discovered that the person you love is unwilling to cooperate in developing a solid relationship, or that you are both unwilling to give to the relationship what the other wants most. And you have gained some closure on the past by forgiving your beloved and by accepting the reality of your situation.

Affirmation of Faith

My faith in God is strong, because it is based on the Word of God. Repeat this affirmation several times a day. It is based on the following Scriptures:

Hebrews 11:1—*Now faith is the assurance of things hoped for, the conviction of things not seen* (*NASB*).

Galatians 5:5—*For we through the Spirit, by faith, are waiting for the hope of righteousness* (*NASB*).

Galatians 2:20—*I am crucified with Christ; nevertheless I live; yet not I, but Christ liveth in me: and the life which I now live in the flesh I live by the faith of the Son of God, who loved me, and gave himself for me* (*KJV*).

CHAPTER THREE

WISHING I WERE DEAD

Your attempts to reconcile the relationship with your beloved have failed and you're beginning to consider the idea that maybe he/she will never come back, that the relationship is ended. Perhaps your divorce is now final, or the love of your life has fallen in love with someone else, or moved away (without leaving a forwarding address).

When you think of the future without your beloved, and everything you're going to have to change about your life-style now that he/she has left, you may feel that if this is *life* then you aren't too thrilled about living. Maybe you are tempted to consider ending your life by committing suicide. This is normal.

Most people have thoughts of suicide after the loss of a love relationship, particularly when they first recognize that all hope for a reconciliation is apparently futile. There are a lot of reasons that people get to the point of contemplating suicide. During the next few weeks, if you work through the specific tasks outlined in this book, you will find that your desires to end it all will leave you because you are cured of your addiction to your beloved. Your hurt will be healed.

Stay Alive

But right now, you hurt. Your basic need is to get through this period and to keep yourself alive. If you are preoccupied with the thought of committing suicide, take *immediate* steps to prevent yourself from actually doing so in a weak moment of despair.

1. *Make it hard to take your own life.* Most people contemplating suicide have a preferred scenario or method for the act. Take steps to put the means for following through with your scenario outside of your control for this short time period. Depending on your fantasy:

—Flush down the toilet such things as poisons, drugs, sleeping pills, tranquilizers.

—Give your razor, blades and guns to a friend who will promise not to let you have them back for several weeks.

—Stay away from cliffs, roofs, top floors of tall buildings.

—Avoid driving alone (car-pool or take the bus to work, and have a friend hold the keys to your car).

—Have the gas turned off in your home.

—Don't go swimming alone, or to the ocean or river.

—Avoid walking across bridges.

2. *Keep emergency phone numbers near your telephone.* Your list might include your family, your pastor, three or four close friends, your coun-

selor, the local crisis line, and even the police. Confess your thoughts of suicide to your family and close friends and explain that you need their help just now. You need to feel free to call one of them in the middle of the night if you feel unable to withstand the temptation to end it all. Ask them to pray for you several times a day during this time.

Decide that if the compulsion to follow through with the idea of suicide ever gets too strong, you will make certain phone calls first. *You must make these calls before doing anything else.* For example, determine that you must talk to two friends, your pastor, your counselor and a member of your family. (You decide on whom you must contact, but the purpose of these conversations is to keep you from suicide.) Tell the people you call where you are, how you feel and ask them to help you to not kill yourself.

3. *Avoid being alone during the time of day when your desire for death is the strongest.* Go to visit or stay overnight with friends, have a friend come stay with you, or go out to a movie, to church, to a singles' function, or to a sports event. You don't have to *want* to go out or to enjoy yourself; your purpose is just to stay alive.

Remember that. Stay alive right now—even if you don't want to or see any reason to. You can always change your mind later, but if you were to kill yourself, there would be no opportunity to change your mind afterwards! Perhaps you haven't had a strong compulsion to commit suicide or made specific plans to do so, but you have entertained the idea or made some vague plans. If so, immediately take the above steps to prevent yourself from following through with those plans.

Understand Why the Idea of Suicide Appeals to You

The idea of suicide may appeal to you for several reasons: because life has no meaning, because you could escape the harsh realities, or because your beloved would suffer. Unfortunately, your thinking is not clear at this point and your judgment is not to be trusted. Instead of dwelling on the possibilities of suicide, consider how you got to this point and what you can do to alleviate your pain.

1. *Rebuild some neglected relationships.* In a romantic relationship you tend to make your beloved the central figure in your life. All events, activities, interests, and other people revolve around him/her in concentric circles of descending priorities in your mind.

You tend to give more and more time and attention to your relationship with your beloved because the emotional payoff of that interaction far surpasses that of any other relationship at the time. This behavior is reinforced by the fact that as the other relationships become less important, the beloved becomes even more significant and essential to your happiness. However, often when lower priorities are neglected for a prolonged period of time, serious problems develop, as in Ellen's case.

When Ellen, 26, fell in love with Fred, she naturally began spending more time with him than with any of her other friends. She found that some of the things which had formerly taken up a lot of her time were less important now. So, if Fred wanted to go out she would skip choir practice on Thursdays, or art class on Mondays. She no longer found time to volunteer at a local nursing home on weekends, and began accepting invitations from girl friends on a tentative basis (OK, unless Fred had other plans for the two of them).

Because, by her actions, she gave these other relationships and activities a lower priority in her life, her friends did the same to their relationships with her. The invitations became fewer, because the likelihood of Ellen's accepting was slim.

For a while Ellen thought everything was terrific, until Fred told Ellen he didn't want an exclusive relationship with her and thought they should both date other people. Panicked at the thought of losing him, Ellen spent weeks trying to "win" Fred back. Nothing else was of any importance right then. When Fred finally explained that he had fallen in love with another woman and that they were getting married right away, Ellen realized that Fred was not going to come back into her life. She was all alone.

Hanging up the phone after talking with Fred for the last time, Ellen took a good look around and burst into tears.

—Her plants had all died. (Who could remember to water plants at a time like this?)

—The Easter Cantata was tomorrow night and she wouldn't be singing. (No time for choir practice lately.)

—There were no invitations for the weekend, and the three friends she called had other plans. ("We had no idea you'd be available, Ellen. Sorry.")

Ellen felt abandoned not only by Fred but also by the rest of her world—because she had "abandoned" her world earlier.

Ellen's story is by no means unique, because many people place a priority on love and will sacrifice a lot to save a love relationship. If this is where you are right now, you may feel not only abandoned but also overwhelmed by the myriad of problems facing you. It may seem as if everything suddenly decided to go wrong, when actually things have been breaking down and piling up for quite some time because you haven't had time for mundane tasks and normal problems.

So now your lawn mower is broken and has to be taken into the shop, the backyard looks like a jungle, the flower gardens are filled with weeds, you have to drive the kids to school for three weeks in a row (you traded with three other parents so you could have three weeks off, remember?), your children aren't getting along with the neighbors, the carpets need cleaning, your bills are unpaid and checkbook unbalanced, and there's no food in the house (who's had time to shop?)!

Even the thought of tackling the tasks facing you makes you tired. The job may seem hopeless. But you can't catch up on weeks (maybe months) of neglect in a few days, so don't even try. Instead, organize the task and approach it systematically. List all of the chores and problems facing you. Choose several easy ones to accomplish first. Water the dying plants, or toss the dead ones out. Clean the house, or hire someone to come in and clean the house and/or carpets. Take the lawn mower to the shop, the cleaning to the dry cleaners and the donation to the local thrift shop.

Do one or two of the other chores on your list each day. You don't need to accomplish miracles, but you must accomplish something every day. Keep your list and mark off the tasks you complete or problems you solve. The crossed-off items on your list will reinforce your sense of achievement. You can see the order you are bringing back into your life. You are regaining control of your world.

It's important that you recognize that you do have control of your life, because inherent in the rejection experience is a feeling of helplessness. Nothing you are doing has influenced your beloved to return to you. Being extra sweet, giving in to demands, sending cards or gifts, making midnight phone calls to your beloved, going out with someone else to try and make your beloved jealous, praying, arguing, crying, threatening, counter-rejection, being loving—all of your efforts have been ignored or ineffective. The truth is: *You cannot make the other person love you.*

By regaining control in your life, you will be able to isolate the helpless feeling to the area of the lost relationship and not let it permeate your entire self-concept.

2. *Look for affirmation.* It's OK to need comfort sometimes. You've suffered an emotional injury and need to be taken care of. Accepting comfort may not be easy for you if you are a strong person who usually gives to rather than receives from others. But allow yourself to be comforted.

You are probably suffering from a desperate need for several types of affirmation. These might include: compliments, recognition, attention, appreciation, sharing affection, touching, loving and sex. If the love of your life was your sole source of these things, you are probably feeling absolutely starved for affirmation. Also, right now, since the most important person in the world has stopped loving you, the love and attention you receive from other people is probably of little value to you.

Cristen explains, "I'm a very touching person. I hug my friends all of the time. But now that Mark and I have split up, I find that when people hug me, I almost pull away. It's Mark's arms I want around me, not theirs. And when a friend tells me that I'm a nice person, I think, 'Oh, yeah! Then why did Mark leave?' I don't know what to do!"

Even if the affirmation of others is not what you want right now, build that love and attention into your life. Go to small group sessions which might be sponsored by your church, a singles ministry, self-help organizations or a counseling center. Share with your family and friends about the positive things you are accomplishing every day— even if you don't feel they are very important right now. Take extra care with your appearance and accept compliments graciously. Learn to be a "toucher." Substitute a warm bear hug for a handshake when greeting your friends (both sexes) and family.

Select several close friends who can be instant affirmers and keep their numbers near your telephone and on a card in your wallet for quick reference when you need contact with someone who cares.

Be nice to yourself. Do things which feel good on a sensory level. Eat your favorite foods. Wear a nice cologne, spray the house with fresh scents, burn incense, or open your jar of potpourri, buy scented soaps. Rub lotion on your skin and lie in the sun. Take a warm bubble bath. Buy satin sheets to sleep on. Decide what materials make you feel special and choose clothes made from those fabrics (a velvet bathrobe, a real silk shirt/blouse). Listen to classical music, hang wind chimes on the patio, or go to a concert. Buy a picture for your bedroom wall, or paint the living room a new color. Go visit your favorite spot outdoors and enjoy yourself.

Of course, doing these things for yourself and by yourself is not as satisfying as being loved by the one you love. These are poor substitutes. *But they are substitutes.* A hungry person may crave steak and lobster, but vegetable soup is better than starvation! And substituted affirmation is better than starving yourself to the point of being ready to die from a lack of love.

An area which is often a major problem at this point is a desire for an intimate relationship with a person of the opposite sex. Because sexual intercourse was designed by God as the ultimate intimacy between a husband and wife, and is not only physically but also emotionally and spiritually satisfying, people who are suffering from rejection may be tempted to become preoccupied with sex and consider casual sex as a way to regain the intimacy they have lost in their lives. The temptation is particularly strong when the people involved have been married before, or if the couple were sexually active.

There are other reasons people give in to the temptation to disobey God's rules for sexual conduct. Patricia says, "My husband had been having an affair during our marriage. When we were divorced, I wanted to go out and show him I could have one too!"

Carl confesses, "When my wife left me, I used

sex to kill the pain. Whenever I was hurting so bad I thought I couldn't stand it anymore, I'd go out with some woman and go to bed with her. It didn't work, I discovered. I felt worse afterwards."

Judy admits, "When my husband asked for a divorce he said he was gay and was going to live with another man. I was shocked and devastated. Immediately I went out and had several sexual encounters to somehow prove that his problem wasn't my fault."

Inevitably, people who try to fulfill their deep needs for love, affirmation and intimacy through casual sexual activity discover that they have sacrificed much (their morals, self-respect, and reputation) and gained nothing. The momentary physical sensation has brought no emotional relief. In fact, the pain may even be greater than before.

Obviously, people who have been used to meeting their sexual needs/desires by having intercourse in the love relationship will experience a need for physical relief when sexual tensions build up. Some people find that cold showers, strenuous physical activity and avoiding things/situations which are sexually stimulating alleviate the problem significantly. Others claim that they resist the temptation to go out and have intercourse by getting physical relief through masturbation.

Instead of having an increased sexual drive, some people respond to abandonment by losing all interest in sex. Either of these extreme responses is normal and will not persist over a long period of time. If all you think of is sex, you may soon be concerned with other things again. If you aren't interested in sex now, you will be again soon.

3. *Take a look at how you perceive your loved*

one. If you believe that your loved one is the *one and only* person in the world for you, then your loss will seem greater than it really is. Not only do you feel that you have lost the most important relationship in your life and the most significant source of affirmation, but you may also believe that by losing your *one and only*, you are now doomed to a life of loneliness. Not so!

There are other people in the world who have similar characteristics as those you admired in the person you love. In fact, because people in love tend to look for interests they have in common and characteristics they admire, and to discount the others, your concept of the person you love is probably a bit one-sided.

Mr. Perfect and Ms. Ideal do not actually exist!

Take time to consider your beloved realistically. Rate him/her using the following list of strengths and weaknesses. (Note that the strength in the first column, when exaggerated or carried to extremes, turns into the corresponding weakness in the second column.)

STRENGTHS	WEAKNESSES
Accepting	Indulgent
Idealistic	Impractical
Receptive	Passive
Seeks excellence	Perfectionist
Self-confident	Arrogant
Forceful	Coercive
Enterprising	Opportunistic
Responds to challenge	Constantly proving self
Tenacious	Cannot let go
Realistic	Unimaginative
Flexible	Inconsistent

Enthusiastic	Agitated
Tactful	Overagreeable
Adaptable	Lacks conviction
Sociable	Unable to be alone
Generous	Spendthrift

Consider which of these characteristics you might have ignored during the relationship. Were these weaknesses something your friends tried to point out to you but you chose to deny? Were there other things about your beloved (idiosyncracies or mannerisms) which you pretended to yourself weren't a problem but were secretly irritating?

Write a description of the person you love, attempting to be as objective as possible. Include strengths, weaknesses, achievements and failures, what they contributed to your relationship and what they took from it or asked of you. Be as detailed as possible. Write until you're too tired to write anymore. Continue at a later time rather than be brief.

As you develop a more realistic perspective of the person you love, you will speed up the disillusionment process and your healing as well.

The next step is to begin to break the dependency ties you built up during your relationship. Did he take care of your car? Did she do your laundry? Did he baby-sit your dog when you went out of town on business trips? Was she the only person with whom you could discuss poetry? List all of the things for which you depended on your beloved and identify two or three ways you can meet those needs without that person. Soon you will feel good about your ability to get along on your own, even if you do still miss your beloved.

4. *Find a safe way to vent your anger and*

desire to punish someone. You have been rejected and may consider suicide as a viable alternative. Your anger might be self-directed—"How could I have been stupid enough to have trusted him?"— or other-directed—"How could she reject me after all we have shared together?"

Harry shares about his attempted suicide several years ago. "My wife, Grace, had divorced me and married my best friend. All I could think about was killing myself so they would feel guilty. I wanted to hurt them as much as they had hurt me."

Sharon says, "I was so depressed I didn't want to live. The one thing that stopped me was that I knew that if I killed myself, instead of feeling sorry for me, my ex-husband would feel that my suicide proved his leaving was justified. I mean, who wants to live with a person who's unstable enough to kill herself?"

Sharon was very perceptive for being depressed. Your suicide would only justify your beloved's leaving you. You have little chance at making your beloved feel guilty for very long by ending your life. And even if you succeeded in making that person feel guilty forever, what have you gained? Your life is worth more than that!

A desire to punish the person who has hurt you is a strong indication that you are having difficulty valuing that person and letting go of your demands of the person you loved. You have not yet come to the point of forgiving the past because you want restitution or vindication in some way. Pray about your secret desires to "hit back" and ask God to help you respond as a Christian should.

Read about Jesus' rejection experiences in

Luke, chapters 22 and 23.

In Luke	*He was . . .*
22:47-53	—betrayed by a friend
22:54-62	—rejected by a close friend
22:63-65	—injured and falsely accused by strangers
22:66—23:26	—unrecognized by leaders
23:27-34	—crucified between sinners
23:35	—mocked by the crowd
23:46-49	—deserted by friends, family and acquaintances

How does your experience relate to His? Write a letter to God expressing your feelings and thoughts at this point.

Another consideration is that instead of punishing the one you'd like to punish by killing yourself, the people who might suffer are your parents, close friends and your children. Are you genuinely ready to inflict the pain of abandonment, which you are now suffering, on those who do still love you? Think of them.

5. *Remove constant reminders of your loved one.* You are surrounded by reminders of the person you love which rekindles your depression. His photograph. Her birthday gift. The souvenir you purchased together on a special trip. The furniture you picked out together. The ugly ceramic figurine you used to argue about because you loved it but your beloved hated it. The outfit in your closet which was your love's favorite. It's no wonder that your love and your loss are uppermost in your thoughts.

The most positive thing you can do right now is to remove all of these reminders from your sight.

Go to the grocery store and pick up one (or more) large cardboard box(es) and start packing a "memory box."

Don't throw or give these things away just now. Pack away anything that reminds you of your beloved. Include clothes, jewelry, perfume, cologne, gifts, cards, photographs (check your wallet), diaries, love letters, books, newspaper clippings, mementos (corsages, stuffed animals, souvenirs, matchbooks). Your home may look stripped when you have finished, but that's OK for now. Put the box(es) in an out-of-the-way place where you aren't always stumbling over it (them). Hide large items in a little-used closet or corner of the garage.

When you go shopping, you may find a friendship card which seems to say exactly what you want to say to your love. Go ahead and buy it—but don't mail it. Put it into your memory box instead. Or perhaps it isn't a card you buy, but a record or gift you'd like to give your beloved. Into the box with it.

Next, change your surroundings even more by rearranging the furniture in a brand new way so you aren't always picturing your beloved "over in that corner sitting in his/her favorite chair." If there was a "favorite chair" and you can't move it to the garage, cover it with a bright new throw to disguise it. If you are a woman, make your home more feminine. Add bright colors, frills, fluffy pillows and flowers. If you are a man, get rid of the feminine frills and give your home an intensely masculine appearance.

You will also want to avoid music which makes you sad. Don't listen to "your song." Avoid country-western and soft-rock songs which are often about lost loves. Instead, listen to Christian music and gospel songs which will remind you of God's love and the fellowship of believers. Or tune your radio to stations which offer news, sports, classical music or even jazz.

Don't spend long afternoons visiting "your special places." You'll only feel worse. Go to new places (restaurants, movies, parks, stores) instead.

Sometimes the biggest problem is people, not things or places. Nelson agrees. "Everywhere I went, it seemed as if people were talking about Helen. Either I was being asked about her or told how/what she was doing. Finally I just started telling people I didn't want to discuss Helen. It took a while, but finally they got the message."

Nelson had the right idea. There's no reason for you to increase your pain by constantly being reminded of the person who walked out on you. You might even want to run away for a while by taking a short trip or a long vacation or going home to visit your family. If you can afford to do so, go ahead—but remember, don't take a trip to a romantic place which you and your beloved used to talk of seeing together; that will only make you feel worse! Make your plans wisely and choose a traveling companion who won't let you give in to your depression. Remember, you will be taking your pain with you.

You may consider moving away. Don't do this right away. Any change in your life increases your stress and the rejection experience is severe enough without adding multiple changes, such as moving to a new city, finding a new home church, making new friends, and starting a new job. Wait a while before you move.

6. *Avoid getting lonely.* Everyone knows that being lonely and being alone are two completely different things. You can be alone and not be lonely; you can be married or be with friends and still feel lonely. A person is lonely to the degree that he/she perceives a lack of *essential* emotional/psychological support. It is more than someone's presence or company which you desire; it is their affirmation of your self-worth. Thus, people with very healthy and positive self-images tend to be less lonely than those whose self-concepts are weak and who depend on others for affirmation.

Whenever a source of love and attention is removed from your life, loneliness is the natural result, and that loneliness can be emphasized and exaggerated if you are also physically alone. So, while your long-range goal will be to find new sources of emotional and psychological strength, your immediate need is to not spend too much time alone.

Fill your schedule so full that you have little time for brooding. Get involved in church activities, classes, volunteer projects, the PTA, community efforts and organizations, singles groups, sports, clubs, or grass-roots politics.

Tackle back-burner projects—things you've always meant to do but have never had time for. Experiment with painting, crafts, rug weaving, cabinet building, or some other time-consuming project which will require your concentration.

Explore any special talents or gifts you have: writing, singing, drawing, or playing a musical instrument.

Expand your social life. Give parties. Go to parties. Cook meals for some of your friends. Celebrate holidays. Get reacquainted with your family (parents, siblings, cousins, aunts and uncles).

Reach out to other people who are lonely and help them overcome their loneliness. Share ideas. Exchange phone numbers and agree to be a prayer partner for them during this period of loneliness.

Try to do at least two nice, thoughtful or kind deeds each day. Keep a private record of these good deeds, not to show to anyone else but to reflect on whenever you experience a sense of worthlessness. Remember how important little kindnesses have sometimes been to you? That's how significant your thoughtfulness can be to someone else.

Surround yourself with living things rather than retreating from life! Fill your living room with plants or put in a backyard garden, get a bird, a few goldfish, a cat or that puppy you've always wanted. Taking care of living things will remind you of the preciousness of life.

Maintaining this type of schedule takes an incredible amount of energy, so you should be exhausted by the time you finally get to bed at night, and falling asleep should be easy. But if you find that you still cannot sleep (or that you awake in the early morning hours and cannot go back to sleep) then don't fight it. Get up. Tossing and turning in bed telling yourself you *absolutely must* get some sleep only makes things worse, as most insomniacs know. Use those wakeful hours doing something which will make you feel good. Read your Bible, read other books, do a load of washing, clean house, go grocery shopping at a 24-hour store, have a cup of coffee at an all-night restaurant, listen to music, watch television, call a friend, or work on a project. When you feel sleepy, return to bed. If you stay up all night, that's alright also—you'll be extra tired the next night.

Keeping busy and avoiding being alone is only an emergency first-aid treatment for the initial pain of loneliness. It is neither the long-range solution nor the cure. The secret to overcoming loneliness is two-fold: First you must develop psychological and emotional inner strength so that, while external support is very important, it is not absolutely essential to your life; second, you need to develop a network of supportive friends who will supply the love and attention you do need. You can't depend on only one person to provide all of your affirmation needs.

But developing inner strength and a supportive network takes time, so for right now, chase loneliness away by keeping busy.

Subtle Suicide

Suicide is defined as the intentional act of taking one's own life, or of destroying one's interests or prospects in life. People who would never seriously consider killing themselves are, however, often guilty of the more subtle forms of suicide. What about you?

Are you *jeopardizing your health* through neglect or dangerous activities involving unnecessary risks?

Are you *committing career suicide* by neglecting your job, failing to show up or being chronically tardy?

Is your *social life* dying because you are cutting people off, failing to keep commitments, being rude or obnoxious or refusing to talk?

Have you decided to "*protect yourself*" from further hurt by refusing to feel anything ever again?

Are you choosing *psychological suicide*—by assuming all of the blame for the failure of the relationship, by putting yourself down, harboring negative attitudes, giving into fear and depression, and by reinforcing a poor self-image?

Have you *ignored your spiritual life*, stopped going to church, reading God's Word, praying, fellowshiping with other believers, and walking by faith?

If so, you will want to begin reversing your attitudes and actions and discontinue your self-destructive patterns.

Establish a pattern of Scripture reading and stick to your plan. Read a portion of the Word every day and ask the Holy Spirit to make God's message come alive in your life. You might read the book of Psalms. David knew not only the joy of victory, but also the pain of rejection, and in his writings he dared to share his pain, his doubts and fears. As you meditate on his writings, you will find not a pious message from a perfect prophet, but a personal comfort from a fellow sufferer—and conqueror!

Suicide vs. Self-Esteem

Basically, suicide is a public statement of a low self-esteem. The message is that the person felt unloved, unwanted, and unnecessary and placed little value on him/herself.

A low self-esteem can be reversed. Most of the action suggestions in this chapter are steps in that direction. You will feel better about yourself as you regain control of your life, develop new sources of affirmation, set and begin accomplishing your goals, revise your concept of the person you love, reduce the number of reminders of your loss, develop ways to cope with loneliness, and break the dependency ties to the one who deserted you.

The important thing to remember is that your own concept of yourself is what counts the most in the area of self-esteem. If you know you are extremely intelligent, it doesn't matter who says you are stupid. But if you believe that you are stupid, it doesn't mean much if someone tells you that you are intelligent! What counts is what you believe! So work on changing your own assessment of yourself. When you believe that you are a person of infinite worth, even the rejection of that worth by a loved one will not cause you to consider suicide as an option.

Seek Professional Help

During this period of time your reaction to being rejected may be extremely serious. Don't be hesitant to seek professional help if needed. You're worth it.

You may have an exaggerated sense of fear. Your behavior may be hysterical, erratic or dangerously self-destructive. Your depression may be too intense for you to cope alone. A trained, Christian counselor can help you survive this painful experience.

Affirmation of Growth

I thank God daily for what He's accomplishing in my life. Repeat this affirmation several times a day. It is based on the following Scripture verses:

   1 Thessalonians 5:18—*In every thing give thanks; for this is the will of God in Christ Jesus concerning you (KJV).*

   Philippians 1:6—*For I am confident of this very thing, that He who began a good work in you will perfect it until the day of Christ Jesus (NASB).*

CHAPTER FOUR

CRYING ALL OF THE TIME

You've suffered the shock of abandonment and your response has ranged from positive hopes of reconciliation to the despair of wanting to end the pain by committing suicide. Now, having faced the facts that a reconciliation is not likely, and suicide is not a solution, you are left to work through your pain some other way.

A deep sadness invades your life. Few situations seem humorous. Daily tasks appear either trivial or monumental. Throughout the day your thoughts stray to the person you love and you start (or feel like starting) to cry.

Julie discovered that during the week she managed to crowd out thoughts of her former husband by keeping busy, avoiding being alone and studying her college homework each night. But on Sunday mornings, sitting quietly in church waiting for the worship service to begin, she would experience a rush of sadness and tears would rain down her face.

Walter's eyes would fill with tears at unexpected moments, driving down the freeway, walking into a crowded room, hearing a song, or seeing a particularly tender commercial on television.

It's embarrassing, annoying and depressing to feel so out of control that you never know when you'll need a box of tissues!

You can gain control.

Your sadness is being triggered by your thoughts. Even though you have eliminated many of the physical reminders of your love, your mind continues to supply almost continual reminders. Suddenly virtually everything you see or every situation you experience is mentally linked to the person who rejected you. Things you never noticed before now have the power to evoke tears. The billboard advertising a major airline which you drive past every day to work now reminds you that you and the one you loved will never take another trip together. A commercial on television, where a spouse goes out in the rain to get cold medicine for the other, triggers the thought that you have no one to care for you when you're sick, and you burst into tears.

Take charge of your thoughts! It is time for action!

Interrupt Your Thoughts

Controlling your thoughts by choosing not to think about the one who rejected you is your goal. And you will soon achieve that goal. But right now you may need to use a few behavioral therapy techniques to interrupt your constant thoughts about that person.

If you are alone and you suddenly start thinking of the one who's making you sad, try one or more of these techniques:

—Yell "NO" as loudly as you can.

—Clap your hands.

—Stamp your foot.

—Slam a door.

—Stop what you're doing, get up and change chairs, or walk to another location in the room.

If you are not alone, you can:

—Pinch yourself.

—Snap a rubber band you are wearing around your wrist.

—Snap your fingers.

—Bite your tongue or lip.

—Tug your earlobe.

—Rub your nose.

—Clench your fists.

Each time you use one of these techniques, also tell yourself, "*I will not think about him/her. These thoughts are not what God wants me to concentrate on.*" (See Philippians 4:8.)

At first you may have to consciously interrupt your sad thoughts, using one of these techniques, several times an hour. But within a few days you will discover that you are gaining control over your thought life, which is one of the goals God has for Christians. (See 2 Corinthians 10:5b.)

You can increase the effectiveness of this technique by deliberately thinking of your beloved at least ten times a day. Then the split second you start to think of that person, use one of the thought-stopping techniques listed above.

Identify Hidden Feelings

Psychologists often describe depression as

anger that is directed at yourself, perhaps in lieu of acknowledging that you are actually angry with someone else. Check the following comparison of thoughts and feelings.

This depressive thought . . .	*might actually be this angry idea*
How could I have been so gullible?	How could he have led me on?
Why wasn't I good enough for her?	Why didn't she recognize how good I was?
I am unlovable.	He's unloving.
I didn't give enough of myself.	She didn't appreciate all that I did give.
I wasn't always kind enough.	He was often rude, or thoughtless.
It's all my fault and I deserve to be abandoned.	She was partly responsible for the failure of our relationship, yet she doesn't even care.
I would never leave him.	He rejected me.

You are probably not consciously feeling angry toward the one you loved because the irritation you might have experienced at any habits or characteristics of that person seems so insignificant when compared with the pain you are suffering now. But in order to get through this stage of your healing you need to identify these hidden feelings.

Sit quietly and allow your mind to search out any angry thoughts and feelings you have been harboring. Express them aloud or in writing. If you find it difficult to think of any angry feelings, then list your sad feelings and thoughts. Next, try to rephrase those thoughts or feelings into angry ones. Read what you have written and see if that is partly what you have been thinking or feeling.

Another way to search out hidden, angry feelings is to ask (and answer) this question: *"If I were angry, it would be because of . . ."* (Or, *"If I were angry, I would feel . . ."*).

Confess these thoughts and feelings to God and commit yourself to forgiving and letting them go. Keeping them inside only prolongs your pain. Acknowledging anger toward the one who hurt you helps you accept the reality that you are not totally at fault in this situation. When you are depressed it is easy to assume a burden of exaggerated guilt and to completely exonerate the other person. Trying to function under a load of assumed guilt is impossible and leads to further depression. Realistically acknowledging one's own faults and working toward overcoming them is rewarding.

Redirect Your Hopes

Hope is tough to kill; as the saying goes, "Hope springs eternal!"

We hope even after recognizing that all hope is gone.

We hope long after everyone else has given up.

And then we continue to hope secretly when we're too embarrassed to admit it.

Because hope can live with virtually no reinforcement it is important that you refuse to allow yourself even the slightest encouragement at this point. Temporarily sever contact with the one you loved, and avoid gossiping or listening to gossip about that person. (If the person who rejected you is your former spouse, and you have children, you may find it a little difficult to avoid contact, especially if the children are in touch with—or visit—

both parents. But, if possible, work out a temporary solution which will allow you some space for getting your life back together.) Later you will want to reconnect with the person you loved, but just now, time apart is what you need, because:

—If he/she is kind or sweet to you, you will continue hoping. (Maybe that person is only being nice to you out of guilt or pity, or because having someone like you still loving after being rejected, feeds his/her ego!)

—If he/she is not kind, you will feel even more sad.

—If you hear that he/she is miserable, you will start hoping for a reconciliation again.

—If you hear that he/she is having a wonderful time, your sadness will be intensified.

So, for now, don't go to parties or groups where you are likely to encounter the person you loved. Be assertive when people start to talk about that person. No matter how hard your heart starts to pound or how many chills go up and down your spine at the mention of your favorite name, politely stop the conversation. Say, "I really do not want to talk (or hear) about that." And don't!

Even without such reinforcement, giving up hope is virtually impossible. Replacing the dream is a better alternative. Now is the time to create a new future, not to recreate the past. Think of all you have learned from your past relationships. You are more experienced. You are more mature and sensitive than before. You are wiser.

"I don't want a better relationship," David asserted sadly, "I just want Eileen back."

That's natural. But begin to visualize a new relationship—even if you don't want another one as long as you live.

Indulge in a little romantic fantasy. Consider an ideal relationship which draws from the good elements you've experienced in past relationships and adds new dimensions never before shared. Plan how you can develop the skills to build a solid relationship such as the one you have dreamed up. Practice listening, or being assertive, if those are the skills you need to develop. Begin replacing thoughts of your past relationship with plans for future ones, and your depression will slip away.

If something happens that tends to reinforce your hope for a reconciliation, apply it to your new dream rather than to the old. For example, if you hear that your ex (boyfriend/girl friend, or spouse) said you were a terrific person, instead of responding by immediately hoping for a reconciliation, respond by acknowledging this affirmation as a sign that you are able to have a good, new relationship with someone.

Remember that by refusing to sit around hoping for a reconciliation and by starting to actively hope for a new relationship, *you are not preventing a reconciliation from occurring*. If the person you loved ever decides to come back to you and rekindle your relationship, you are free to respond. But right now, waiting for the past will only immobilize you, while hoping for the future sets you free to live the present.

Imagine the relationship you and your ex had as an isolated geographic location. The one you loved has walked away, back toward civilization. You have stayed, waiting, crying, mourning and hoping for your ex to return. You can spend the rest of your life out there waiting. Or you can choose to leave that once-special place behind and walk back toward life. Being left is not enough to set you free; you must decidedly walk away, leaving the past behind if you are to be healed.

It may seem unthinkable to give up hoping that the person who left you will someday return, to know that your whole investment is lost. But there comes a time when you decide that this relationship is truly over and you will no longer invest any more in it. No more time, energy, self-respect, emotion, hope or tears. No more of your life.

Write the "Last Love Letter"

Dr. Zev Wanderer suggests writing a long, last love letter to your ex. Use this letter to record all of your thoughts, feelings, hopes and dreams. *This letter will not be mailed.* It is only a technique to help you express all of the things you want to say to (or about) your ex but can't because you have temporarily severed communications with (or about) that person. (If you hate writing, you might use a tape recorder for this exercise.)

Your "letter" might include: ideas about how the two of you could make the relationship work, apologies, confessions, longings, fears, fantasies, memories of the good times you shared, reports of daily happenings you'd like to share.

Your "letter" will be a running record of your thoughts. Add paragraphs at any time during the day when you think of something you simply "must tell" your ex. Writing (or recording) those ideas lets you forget them rather than carrying them around in your head all day long.

Have a Daily Pity Party

This is one of the few times in life when having *pity parties* (wallowing in self-pity) is recommended. Usually, focusing on feeling sad is less productive than taking positive action to achieving a goal or accomplishing a task. But when you have lost a significant other from your life, you need to experience grief as part of the mourning process. Your healing depends on it.

Psychologists recommend setting aside one hour a day for a *pity party*. Use a kitchen timer, or set the alarm on your clock or watch, so you will be sure to use the full sixty minutes crying and mourning your loss. This is an excellent time to write (or record) your last love letter. To relive your memories. To express your fears or sad thoughts. To confess your anger.

Now that you will have a designated time each day to dwell on your ex, you will find it easier to interrupt those thoughts which are scattered throughout your day by postponing them until that time.

Select a most inconvenient time for your sixty minutes of mourning so you will not look forward to it. Schedule a *pity party* at a time when you would rather be doing something else, such as relaxing, watching a favorite television show, reading, or even sleeping.

Choose an unusual location and uncomfortable situation for this special hour each day. First, if you were to just sit down anywhere in your home to cry, then that chair or room would in the future always remind you of the pain you are now suffering. So the place should be unusual. And, even though spending an hour a day grieving is helpful, it should not be enjoyable. In fact, one of your goals is to associate thinking of your ex with discomfort so you won't be tempted to dwell on the past or your loss. So you will want to set up an uncomfortable, unusual location for your crying time. For example:

—standing up in a corner of a room you don't often use

—sitting cross-legged on the floor of the closet (attic, garage or basement)

—some place too cold or hot to be comfortable

—soaking feet in ice-cold water in the bathroom, or sitting in a bathtub of cold water with your clothes on.

Be creative. Find your own mourning space and position and wallow in self-pity. If you feel angry, beat up on a pillow. Scream. Cry. Verbalize to your imaginary beloved. Write. Relive your memories. Grieve. Imagine your worst fears coming true and how you would react.

Kathy imagined her ex coming back to their house, bringing a new love and introducing her to Kathy. Although the idea was painful, Kathy realized that she could survive such an experience.

Larry imagined himself growing old without ever having another relationship. He imagined years of sitting by a telephone which never rang, and of never receiving any mail. He fantasized himself setting traps for the mail delivery person or making phoney calls for appliance repairs or to the telephone operator just to have someone to talk with. Soon Larry was smiling at his own absurdity.

At first, when you seem to be thinking of the person you loved all day long, every waking minute, limiting your thoughts to only sixty minutes a day seems impossible. But very soon you will begin to have difficulty filling the hour with sad thoughts.

Be sure to spend the full hour grieving for at least one week or the technique will not be effective. After a few days you will think, "I really don't feel like doing this today." If you faithfully stick to the mourning plan, your next thoughts will be stronger: "I'm bored with thinking sad thoughts!" After several more days you may discover yourself thinking, "I hate thinking about the past!" By forcing yourself to indulge in self-pity you will force yourself through the depression you're suffering and onto the next step in the letting-go process.

After a week or two you will find that you can successfully interrupt non-productive thoughts and have no real need for a *pity party* each day.

Affirmation of Thought-Control

My thoughts and attitudes are obedient to God's Word. Repeat this affirmation several times a day. It is based on the following Scriptures:

Romans 12:2a—*Do not conform any longer to the pattern of this world, but be transformed by the renewing of your mind* (NIV).

1 Corinthians 2:16b—*But we have the mind of Christ* (NIV).

2 Corinthians 10:5—*We are destroying speculations and every lofty thing raised up against the knowledge of God, and we are taking every thought captive to the obedience of Christ* (NASB).

CHAPTER FIVE

BREAKING THE ADDICTION

If you have incorporated into your life the therapeutic techniques suggested in the first four chapters, you are most likely no longer suffering from severe depression—at least not every day, all day long.

You are regaining control over the many chores involved with daily living.

You are affirming strength, faith, growth and thought-control in your life each day.

You are meditating on God's Word and talking with God each day.

I Miss the Romance

At this point you may be able to identify with Sandra who shares, "I've come to the realization that Tom will never return to my life. And even if he did I don't think I'd want to get engaged to him again. This isn't the first time we've broken off our relationship; it's the third. Always before, I was willing to get back together again whenever he decided to. But it won't work with us. You know, if I'm honest, it is not Tom I miss right now; it's the romance—having someone special there who cares for me!"

Sometimes we can let go of the person, but letting go of love (false love, romantic love, true love or any kind of love) is frightening. So we cling to the memory of love as if it were the real thing, afraid of the great void which it would leave.

When your ex first left you, the space he/she had occupied in your life filled with shock, hope, pain and depression. You spent your time surviving, trying to win back the one you loved, and grieving. Now that you have regained control of your life and confined the time you spend thinking about that person, you have discovered significant gaps in your day which need to be filled with activities that will make you feel good. You also have discovered times when you yearn to be loved—to have romance in your life once more.

Those yearnings, not surprisingly, may be triggered by the same things which a week or two ago caused you to feel sad or depressed. Now your response is less one of sadness than one of longing. Great! You have begun to believe, deep inside, that there will be a love relationship in your future.

However, because at the moment your most familiar source of romance is the person with whom you were most recently in love with, you will tend to want to turn to that person whenever your desires for romance become too strong to ignore— when you feel a need for a "love-fix."

Use Your Imagination

One of the reasons you want to turn to the person you once loved is that you still view that person as romantic. Use your imagination to conjure up an image of that person which will trigger your sense of the ridiculous and make you laugh at, rather than long for, that person.

If she was a fussy housekeeper, imagine her making mud pies on the living room floor—right on the new white carpet.

Imagine him walking into a business meeting wearing diapers.

Visualize her going into a fancy restaurant in her pajamas and robe, with night cream all over her face.

See him going to work on a moped instead of his favorite Mercedes.

Fantasize about her being surrounded by a thousand cats who are sharing her home—cats in the closets and cupboards, on the tables, sofa, bed, and chairs. Everywhere you look are cats. In order to even talk to her, you would have to crawl over a hundred cats.

Deliberately visualize your ex in a situation which is so out of character that it is ridiculous. At least five times a day evoke the new image of your ex, and learn to laugh.

Don't Indulge

If you give in to your desires to indulge in a "love-fix," and go get some love or attention from your ex, you have only reinforced your addiction. And the more often you indulge in getting "love-fixes," the stronger the addiction. Reformed alcoholics do not stay sober by having just "one little drink" whenever the desire to drink becomes too strong. Neither will you kick your habit by continuing to get periodic reinforcement from your ex.

Of course, you won't find your craving for romance easy to ignore. But you can learn control by delaying gratification of your desires. Waiting an hour to fulfill an urge will temporarily cause the urge to go away. If you walk by a bakery, the delicious smell might give you a strong urge to go off your diet and have some fresh, hot bread. If you decide to wait an hour before eating the bread, the urge will probably be either gone or weakened enough that you can resist temptation.

However, what you do during the hour of waiting will influence whether or not the urge is weakened or strengthened. If you go about your business and keep on walking, running errands, doing your shopping, and stop to eat a salad, you will find the urge to eat fresh bread is resistible. On the other hand, if you stand in front of the bakery, hungrily eyeing the fresh bread and counting the minutes until the hour is up, then you will have little resistance and will most likely indulge your desire for bread.

The same is true when it comes to your desires for a "love-fix." If you sit with your hand on the telephone dial, the urge to call your ex will be as strong, or stronger, by the end of the sixty minutes as it was at the beginning. On the other hand, substituting another action or activity for the one you have an urge to do will help you resist the temptation to indulge the urge.

You will be even more successful in resisting temptation if you substitute some activity which is very special for you and would actually reward you for denying the impulse to indulge. Only you can determine what an effective substitution would be.

Earl substituted lying out in the backyard in the sun for indulging his urge to call his ex. After a month he not only had succeeded in conquering his addiction to that relationship, but had also developed a gorgeous tan. Earl said he had always wanted to get a tan, but never before had taken time to do so!

Nancy worked on her painting.

Sara gave herself points each time she resisted the urge to contact her ex. The points were worth one dollar each toward the down payment for a new car she wanted.

Caution: Don't substitute a bad habit for the one you are trying to break! Turning to street or prescription drugs, alcohol, cigarettes or food is not the solution to your situation.

A Rainy Day Basket

When you were young did your mother have a "rainy day box" of things for you to do? If so, it may have included unusual activities or games just for those times you couldn't go out to play. Perhaps it wasn't a box so much as it was a plan—permission to do things you were not often allowed to do—picnicking in the living room, baking cream puffs, or talking on the telephone for a whole hour.

It may sound silly, but right now you could have a "rainy day basket" for when you need something special to do instead of giving in to your urge to call your former love. Fill the basket with photos, projects, objects which will make you feel good:

—snapshots of you twenty pounds ago and looking most attractive

—awards, trophies or certificates you have won and are especially proud of

—old mementoes from your teenage years

—treasured letters or autographed photos, books, or records (as long as they aren't from your ex)

—newspaper clippings about you or one of your accomplishments

—special poems or books you enjoy reading

—old yearbooks or autograph books

—your childhood diary.

Or you might choose to include things to do in your basket. Clip newspaper articles about interesting places to see and things to do in your city and save them for possible pursuing on a "rainy day." If your local chamber of commerce or automobile club has a guide to tourist attractions for your area, include this in your basket.

Planning specific things you can do, or having reading material or objects which will make you feel good, is a positive way to prepare for those depressing times which are inevitable when you have been rejected. It's hard to be depressed while watching home movies of yourself as a cute little two-year-old, or while trying to figure out the instructions to a complicated craft project.

Learning that you can control your urge for a "love-fix" will affirm your faith in yourself.

Fill the Empty Spaces

Review chapters 3 and 4 of this book for action suggestions which would help you fill the empty spaces in your life. Establish or strengthen your supportive network, increase the affirmation in your life, work toward goals you have set and explore new activities.

Continue with any of the therapeutic behaviors suggested which are still helpful to you. Spend time completing a spiritual self-assessment to determine in which areas God would have you concentrate your developmental energies at this time.

One way might be to evaluate yourself in relationship to the fruit of the Spirit listed in Galatians 5:22,23. Which of these characteristics are present and which are lacking in your life? (For easy reference, they are: love, joy, peace, patience, kindness, faithfulness, gentleness, and self-control, *NASB*.)

Select one of the characteristics which is not as evident in your life as it should be and do a Scripture word study on it, using a comprehensive Bible concordance. See what God says about that characteristic. Consider ways to develop and grow in that area. Ask God to help you manifest that spiritual characteristic. Chart your progress.

Another helpful assignment is to develop two lists:

1. what I used to expect from my beloved
2. what I used to depend on God for.

Have those lists changed at all in the last month? (For example, if you had written in the first column "to always be with me," would you now move that phrase to the second column?) How would you explain any items in the lists which have changed? Or those which have not?

As you are changing from depending on your ex to depending on God for that which is essential to

your life, you can see that you are healing.
You are overcoming your addiction!

Affirmation of Having Your Needs Met

God knows my needs and will meet those needs because He cares for me.

Repeat this affirmation several times a day. It is based on the following Scriptures:

Philippians 4:19—*And my God shall supply all your needs according to His riches in glory in Christ Jesus (NASB).*

1 Peter 5:7—*Cast all your anxiety on him because he cares for you (NIV).*

CHAPTER SIX

CHASING YOUR FANTASY

As Darlene shared in the small-group discussion session, everyone nodded in self-recognition. Her experience was common to the rejection experience. She was "seeing" her ex everywhere. "I'll be driving down the freeway and see a man in a car up ahead whose hair looks exactly like Bob's," she confesses shyly, "and the next thing I know I'll be following that car, hoping to catch a glimpse of Bob! How stupid! I mean, last time it was a Mercedes I followed, and Bob drives a Volkswagen Rabbit!"

It's not stupid; it is a normal reaction under the circumstances. You've probably had a similar experience. Perhaps it is not the back of a head but a certain breed of dog, or color of car, or shape, or blue suit which you associate with the one you loved. So every time you see one of those things, you have the incredible urge to check it out in case it is your ex. So maybe you've been following cars, checking license plates, tapping strangers on the shoulder, making dangerous U-turns as you're driving, or otherwise making yourself feel foolish.

You know that your ex isn't likely to be everywhere you seem to see him/her, but logic has little to do with this particular hangover effect of having been in love. Henry admitted that even though he knew that his former girl friend had gone to Europe, he still imagined that every blonde with a gorgeous tan he saw was she. His adrenaline level rose; he would immediately imagine that his fantasy had come true—Gloria realized she couldn't live without him and had returned from Europe and was planning to surprise him. They would fall into each other's arms and never be separated again. Even as he would tell himself that he was being silly, Henry would follow the blonde to see if she were Gloria.

Marcia reacted to every male she saw walking a German shepherd dog, even after she heard that her ex-boyfriend had given away his dog.

Neil slowed down every time he passed a tennis court hoping to see his ex-wife, because she was an avid player. He knew that she played only at the country club and never at a park or a high school. Still he looked for her on every court he passed.

"Seeing" your ex everywhere is actually a way of fulfilling your wish to see that person. You hope that somehow your wish has come true and that you have met by chance. You know that if you were to call your ex the outcome would probably not be what you would like, but perhaps if you met accidentally, things would be different. You secretly believe that a chance meeting is your last possibility for a reunion. So when you "see" your ex, you want to make sure you don't miss this last opportunity—you pursue the car, you follow strangers, no matter how embarrassed you get.

Any Blue Bug vs. "The" Blue Bug

In spite of the fact that you are still extra sensitive to anything which reminds you of the one you loved, you need to start distinguishing between *the blue bug* and all other blue Volkswagen bugs. This is important not only to keep you out of embarrassing situations, but also to stop reinforcing your secret fantasy of reunion which plays out mentally each time you imagine that you have accidentally run into your love. Clinging to and feeding false hope is not a healthy approach to coping with rejection.

Dr. Wanderer suggests that you set aside one whole day to prove to your overactive imagination that every woman in a blue bug or every grey-haired man is not your ex. Spend the entire day compulsively checking out whatever it is that has been triggering your fantasy of "seeing" that person everywhere you go. It doesn't matter if you happen to know for a fact that your ex is out of state on that day; you're not pursuing a real person, only a fantasy. In fact, it is better if you can plan for a day when you know that your chances of really meeting your ex are zero.

Go where you usually find yourself looking for your ex—the shopping mall, the grocery store, driving down the freeway, or walking in the park. Walk. Walk. Walk. Look until you are tired of looking. Go from one store to another. Wear yourself out. Each time you see a blue bug or a tan blonde (or whatever), check carefully to prove to yourself that it was not your ex.

If you do meet your ex, don't stop to chat; you have serious work to do today. You are out to discover just how many other people there are in your area who drive the same type of car, own the same breed of dog, or wear their hair the same way as your ex does. If you can convince your senses that they must not respond to all of these other stimuli, you will have let go of one more painful tie to the past.

Part of the secret fantasy is that the beloved is searching for you just as you are searching for that person. Each time you think you have accidentally "found" your ex, and you discover that you haven't, then you experience disappointment and your hopes are dashed. The more times you can experience this disappointment in one day, the quicker you will extinguish your own undesirable habit of responding to *every blue bug* or *every tan blonde*.

Take Pictures

In extreme cases where one day of chasing strange cars, people or animals is not enough to break the response to such generalized stimuli, a second day may be needed. It might be helpful to take along a camera to photograph all of your "suspects." Afterwards, review each photograph carefully to make sure that it was not your ex that you saw. Try to determine what distinguishing characteristics of the car, person, dog should have been your first clue that you were pursuing the wrong person. Analyze each photo carefully.

Keep the photos. Make a collage for your wall or carry them in your purse or car to remind you, the next time some stranger makes you think of your ex, just how unlikely it is for you to accidentally encounter that person.

Regain Your Poise

As long as you are secretly hoping to encounter your ex and are fantasizing about a romantic reunion, you are not likely to react well should you ever meet that person. You might become tongue-tied, or blurt out something which would make you so embarrassed you might not be able to sleep that night.

Carol, surprised at seeing her former boyfriend at the checkout counter, gushed, "Oh, Peter! I've been wanting to talk to you. I've missed you so much. Could you come over tonight for dinner?"

"No. He's busy," answered Rose, his new girl friend, whom Carol hadn't noticed in her eagerness and excitement at seeing Peter again.

Throw away the fantasies and face reality and, in doing so, regain your personal poise for dealing with any situation that arises.

Conduct an Assets Inventory

You really do have the ability to cope with this experience in your life. In fact, you have a great many assets; some you may not have recognized or you may even have forgotten. Take time for a complete self-assessment. Get a paper and pencil and start listing every positive thing about you, from simply being alive to all of your special skills or talents. Don't be modest. Write what would make you interesting to another person. Note your accomplishments.

Here are some ideas to help you get started with your lists. (Be sure to number your assets.)

1. *Physical.* Few people are completely satisfied with their bodies; either the size, shape, height or hair color is perceived as less than satisfactory. Ignore your complaints and itemize your good features. Are your eyes an unusual shade of green? Is your mouth just perfect for your face? Are your teeth pearly white?

If all you can think of are negative observations, then consider each one and turn it into a positive asset. Connie had always hated being short—she was 5'1". Then one day she realized that some people were attracted to her because of her height. She explains, "Paul, this guy I was dating, told me he always felt flattered whenever we talked because I had to look up to him!" The physical act of tilting her head back and looking up came across at a psychological level as an appealing gesture! Many features which people perceive as totally negative turn out to be positive.

Are you in tip-top physical condition? List that. Can you run ten miles or play handball for hours?

2. *Background.* Do you have an intriguing accent, speak a second language, come from another part of the country (or world)? Did your ancestors discover gold in California, or oil in Texas? Are you directly related to any famous persons: historical figures, politicians, movie or television actors or actresses? Your education, trips to other places, or funny memories from your childhood are definitely interesting and have contributed to making you the unique person you are today.

3. *Achievements.* List your awards, certificates, promotions, special appointments or moments which made you proud. The time when

you were twelve and caught the biggest fish. Or when you were selected as an outstanding American.

What dreams have you had in the past and successfully worked to achieve? Dreams needn't be of great significance to be rewarding. Remember how fantastic you felt when you cooked your first meal for the family—or your first meal for yourself after becoming single again? What little things have you accomplished which brought you moments of deep, personal pleasure?

4. *Skills or talents.* Include any special skill you have developed or talents you have. Can you milk a cow? Sing? Write? Play the flute? Quilt? Cook? Sew? Clean house? Repair cars? Baby-sit? Think of all of the things you have learned to do in your lifetime—you are a very talented and highly skilled individual! Don't limit your list to only those things you do well—include everything you know how to do.

5. *Interests.* Hobbies, interests and favorite activities are your next group of assets. Skin diving, tennis, bowling, model building, gardening, walking, cycling, racing, reading, collecting or even shopping are activities which are enjoyed by thousands of people around you. Identify the things you enjoy.

6. *Possessions.* What do you own that might be unusual or interesting? Perhaps you have a rare coin collection, a gold coin from 1800, a Matthew Henry photo of Lincoln, an Indian war club or a new sports car. Walk through your house and itemize those possessions which would fit on your personal assets inventory.

7. *Goals.* One of the most revealing things

about a person is the goals which he/she sets. What are you striving to accomplish? Do you have physical fitness goals? Career goals? Educational goals? Add them to your list.

8. *Characteristics.* Identify those characteristics which are your strengths.

Once you have completed an exhaustive self-assessment, you may be surprised to discover just how many strengths you have and what a fascinating person you actually are. Keep the lists you have made and add to them as you remember other assets.

Use your lists to affirm yourself whenever you are feeling low or downright depressed. Read them aloud. Proudly say each thing you have included. Or record your list on tape, using a bright, bouncy tone—or sing your assets, using a favorite melody. Play the tape back when you need a lift.

Affirmation of Peace

I am at peace because God is in control of my life. Repeat this affirmation several times a day. It is based on the following Scriptures:

Romans 8:6b—*The mind set on the Spirit is life and peace (NASB).*

Philippians 4:7—*And the peace of God, which surpasses all comprehension, shall guard your hearts and your minds in Christ Jesus (NASB).*

CHAPTER SEVEN

WANTING TO GET EVEN

It's now almost two months since the person you loved left you and you may be shocked to discover that your thoughts about that person have changed from hurtful to hateful.

Scott shares, "I started thinking about how I could make my ex-wife suffer. I didn't want her to be happy; she deserved to be miserable. I didn't actually want her back by then, but I didn't want her to be with anyone else either!"

Fay agrees. "I used to have fantasies about winning my former boyfriend back and when I had him hooked, dumping him so that he could see how it felt."

"I considered turning my ex in to the IRS because I knew she had lied on her income tax return," Ryan admits.

Natural Hostility

Angry, vengeful thoughts are not uncommon at this stage of your healing process. When you were first rejected you suppressed any hostile feelings you may have had toward the person you loved for fear that expression of those feelings would result in further alienation. Now that you have worked through some of your pain and have broken the addicting ties between you, your hostile feelings surface. These leftover feelings may be the result of frustration, jealousy, or of feeling betrayed.

1. Frustration. For the last several weeks you have experienced wanting something (being loved) from your former love, and all of your attempts and desires have been frustrated. When someone or something prevents us from reaching a goal, we feel frustrated and powerless. And adults often respond to frustration by throwing tantrums, much like toddlers who stomp on or break a toy they can't get to operate.

An adult tantrum is, of course, more dangerous because, all too often, it is people, not things, who get hurt.

2. Jealousy. Most people have a natural tendency to stake out their territories and label their possessions—including people. Think of how you tend to introduce people by explaining their relationship to you: my husband; my girl friend; my son; my mother; my teacher; or my best friend. And people are usually quite protective of their possessions. If a stranger were to enter your house uninvited and use your toothbrush, eat your food, or steal your car, you would probably feel outraged!

When someone steals your beloved, you experience that same sense of outrage at being ripped off.

What's really important to realize at this point

is that people are not possessions to be owned, and that they cannot be stolen—they choose to walk away. Human beings are agents of free choice. They go or stay by choice. No one can convince someone to leave if that person wants to stay, or to stay if the decision to leave has been made.

Part of your jealous feelings may include the perception that what you always wanted from your ex, and never (or at least not recently) received, is now being freely given to someone else. In Trudy's case, it was travel. She had always tried to talk her husband into taking vacation trips, but he consistently refused and insisted on staying home. For the first six months of his new marriage, he and his second wife were seldom home, taking one trip after another. Trudy was furiously jealous.

Maybe it is love, attention, flowers, companionship—whatever it is you missed in your former relationship—if that is now a reality for the person in your ex's life, you are probably feeling jealous and want to strike out and hurt the one who refused to give you what you wanted, or the one who got whatever it was you wanted.

3. *Feeling betrayed.* Perhaps underlying your anger is a sense of feeling betrayed because the one you trusted with your love turned to someone else. And you torture yourself with thoughts of, "If only I had tried . . ." or "Maybe, I could have been more . . ." Instead, tell yourself, "That new person is offering more than (or something different from) what I wanted to offer."

When Tracy took a realistic view of what her ex-husband's new girl friend was giving him, she laughed at just how hurt she had been feeling. Her husband, 43, had started dating a pretty young girl whose main contribution to the relationship was being totally awed by his vice-president title and thinking that *everything* George said was terribly clever.

Most likely, whatever your ex finds in the new relationship, it is not something you were prepared to give. Did he want a child? Did she want a bigger house? Did he want to spend every weekend golfing? Did she want to spend every evening talking out deep, emotional feelings? Did he want you to quit your job, or go to work? Did she want more freedom? Did he want to come first with you?

Chances are, if you knew what that person wanted, you didn't choose to give it. So, probably the breakup was partly your choice, even if it was only on a subconscious level. However, maybe you didn't know what your former love wanted and would have been willing to give it if you had been asked. In that case your sense of betrayal is probably deep.

In Burt's case, there really was betrayal. His girl friend Alice had fallen in love with another man and, instead of honestly telling Burt, she sabotaged their relationship with criticism and frequent quarrels. Her actions undermined Burt's self-esteem as she made him believe that his inadequacy was the reason their relationship failed. Yet, all along she had planned to leave Burt for someone else.

Whatever elements in your own story make you feel betrayed, you probably have thought of ways to get even with the one who hurt you.

Your natural hostility is a healthy sign that

your anger, which has been self-directed, is now turning toward the appropriate target. Until you recognize and accept that you are angry with the person who hurt you, you are unable to confess that anger and receive healing. As long as you are accepting all of the responsibility and blame for the failure of your relationship, you are refusing to face the truth.

The truth is: *You have been hurt. (And you may have been wronged, betrayed or manipulated.)*

The truth is: *You don't need someone in your life who only causes you pain. It is time to let go.*

Spiritual Victory

Even though anger toward your ex is a natural response in the rejection experience, the scriptural response is to be forgiving. This may seem strange or even impossible, but God's ways are higher than ours. (See 1 Corinthians 2:14-16; Romans 11:33; Isaiah 55:9.) And God's instructions to us are clear:

If you are angry, be sure that it is not out of wounded pride or bad temper. Never go to bed angry—don't give the devil that sort of foothold. . . . Let there be no more resentment, no more anger or temper, no more violent self-assertiveness, no more slander and no more malicious remarks. Be kind to one another; be understanding. Be as ready to forgive others as God for Christ's sake has forgiven you, Ephesians 4:26,27,31,32 *(Phillips).*

Maybe you read those verses and say, "Yes, Lord, but . . .

—I'm not big enough to forgive him."

—You don't know what I've been through."
—There's too much to forgive."
—She's not even sorry."
—He deserves to suffer."

Of course, it is not *natural* to forgive, help and honor those who hurt us. But it is God's way. You might not want to hear that statement. Perhaps you are outraged, thinking, "But I'm the one who has been wronged. Why should I go that extra mile and forgive that person?" Or, "That's not fair!"

I know how you feel. Not long ago, wrestling with anger and hurt, I did a lot of reading and studying about forgiveness and found a sentence which meant a lot to me!

Forgiveness is not a receipt for a payment in full![1]

True forgiveness does not demand restitution, for that is payment of the debt. And if the "debt" is paid, no forgiveness is involved. As we seek to forgive those who have wronged us, we should not try to *understand* the other person; just be *understanding*. If we try to understand we set ourselves up as judges. We'll forgive *if* we think there was a good reason for the action. Instead, we are just to be understanding. The key to doing that is in the concept that *people are coping with life the best way they can*! If they had the ability to cope another way, they would do so. Still, it is hard to be forgiving.

Lately, I've been thinking about this concept and tried to integrate it into my life when I went to visit a friend with a new baby. Sure enough, during the visit the baby wet his diaper and had to be changed. Although few of us would list this as one of life's little pleasures, most of us understand that babies cope with their physical needs the best way they can! A one-month-old baby cannot speak up and say that it has to go to the bathroom. Babies wet their diapers. Sometimes in the process they even ruin someone's new silk dress or shirt.

But I've never seen an adult throw the baby into the crib and scream angrily, "How could you do this to me when all I was doing was loving you?"

Neither have I seen an adult go change the baby's diaper, and then say seriously, "I forgive you for wetting on me!"

What is there to forgive? How do you fault someone for doing the best he can?

Sometimes babies do not mature at the normal rate. They are developmentally disabled. So they don't walk at ten months or talk at two years. They may stay at a one-year developmental level even though they are six (or more) years old. But we don't fault them for not performing at their chronological age level because they haven't developed those skills yet. So if they act like one-year-olds, instead of becoming angry with them or forgiving them, we try to help them to develop two-year-old level skills.

I wonder if this same principle doesn't apply to all of us. We are, none of us, fully mature or perfect. We are developing. Some of us develop faster than others; some grow up much slower than we would wish. But instead of faulting people, what if we looked beyond the behavior and saw the need?

—Is Jack unfaithful because he hasn't learned how to make a commitment?

—Is Jaynie selfish because she hasn't learned to give?

—Did Tom walk out of your relationship

because he felt he couldn't live without more affirmation and attention than you could give him?

—Did Sally reject you because she couldn't face the reality of having to struggle financially?

The reasons don't matter that much because we really can't see inside someone else to determine just why they did what they did. Maybe they don't even know the real *why*. Instead of deciding whether or not your ex had a good reason (by your standards) for behaving in a certain way, just say that he/she left you because he/she was coping the best way he/she could.

I am sure that God looks at me and wishes I were further along in my development toward becoming conformed to the image of Christ than I am. But I also think He is understanding. He knows I'm growing as fast as I can and celebrates each new development and step with me.

This approach to relationships actually works! What a freeing experience not to be bound to the past by the failure to forgive. By forgiving one another, we establish a climate which allows repentance and the restoration of a relationship. Maybe not the intimate or romantic relationship which you used to want from your ex, but a new relationship, a friendship of lasting value.

The challenge to forgive brings with it a spiritual victory over anger. Remember Christ's prayer on the cross, "Father, forgive them, for they know not what they do"? Can you live up to the challenge of forgiving others even as God, for Christ's sake, has forgiven you?

Feeling Powerful

Perhaps you aren't quite ready to let go of your

anger because, secretly, it makes you feel good. One of the most devastating aspects of losing love is feeling powerless. But now your anger has given you a sense of regaining power because you recognize that you have the ability and the means to hurt your ex.

You are losing your victim status.

Unfortunately, you are doing so by assuming another role, that of the prosecutor! In this role you may have fantasized about ways to get even with your ex, or to sabotage the new relationship, or cause all kinds of trouble. You may even dream of killing the person who "ruined your life." Perhaps you have spread gossip about that person, or followed through on one of your other fantasies for revenge. You may have discovered that the more you expressed your anger, the less depressed you became.

Maybe. But if so, you probably also discovered that being angry, entertaining vengeful thoughts and acting out your angry feelings, have left you guilty before God—and feeling worse.

So what are you to do? If you repress anger it turns inward and destroys you or surfaces indirectly and explodes at innocent victims (your children, family, friends). The alternative is to confess those feelings to God. Tell Him all about those fantasies you've been harboring. Verbalizing them will help you get them out of your system. Saying the words aloud is no different than thinking them in your head. God has already heard your thoughts!

Sometimes physical action helps exorcise the dregs of anger you've hidden in your very soul. Beat on a pillow. Tear up a phone book. Stomp.

Pound the sofa. Lie on a bed and kick your feet. Hit a punching bag. Play the piano at full crescendo. Play the drums, loudly. Yell and scream (making sure that you are alone and all the windows are closed; in fact, a closed car works well as a "scream chamber" if you are parked in a deserted area). You may feel silly, but no one is watching, except God, and He understands.

Don't hold back. Ask the Holy Spirit to search your heart and reveal any leftover anger you are not recognizing. Say with David, *Search me, O God, and know my heart; try me and know my anxious thoughts; and see if there be any hurtful way in me, and lead me in the everlasting way* (Psalm 139:23,24, *NASB*).

Then ask God to create a clean heart and a forgiving attitude in you so that you can learn to forgive others—even your ex, in the same way He forgives you.

The real power in an interpersonal conflict is not in having the last word or the last blow, but in rising above the fight and being forgiving. Remember those old movies where the hero, after being engaged in a mortal combat, stands victorious, sword poised on the loser's throat? Remember that moment when the victor magnanimously steps away and spares the victim's life? That's power!

You are not powerless. You are big enough to forgive, and that invests you with incredible power.

Affirmation of Forgiveness
I have a forgiving attitude toward everyone.

Repeat this affirmation several times a day. It is based on the following Scriptures:

Ephesians 4:32—*And be kind to one another, tender-hearted, forgiving each other, just as God in Christ also has forgiven you (NASB).*

Mark 11:25,26—*And whenever you stand praying, forgive, if you have anything against anyone; so that your Father also who is in heaven may forgive you your transgressions. (But if you do not forgive, neither will your Father who is in heaven forgive your transgressions) (NASB).*

Note
1. David Augsburger, *Caring Enough to Forgive*, (Ventura, CA: Regal Books, 1982).

CHAPTER EIGHT
KILLING GHOSTS

Your world is full of ghosts: old memories, special places, familiar sights and smells. Everywhere you turn you are haunted by the past. It's time to confront the ghosts which have been haunting you. Time to kill them off and reclaim your world.

You are now strong enough to face all of those things you've been avoiding because they triggered the pain of sadness, unfulfilled hope, depression or even anger. Your strength has come from spending the last few weeks working through the devastating pain of rejection, from reclaiming control of your life, from building alternate sources of affirmation into your life, and from maintaining a personal relationship with the Lord.

Mourning Day
Set aside one whole day to mourn your lost relationship. Deliberately plan to make this day the saddest of your life. One reason some people carry

a lingering sadness around inside for years is that they never fully mourned their loss. Don't let that happen to you.

1. Set a sad date. Schedule your mourning day on a date that had a special significance in your relationship, such as a holiday, birthday or anniversary, or on that day of the week which you had always reserved for just-the-two-of-you dates.

You are going to spend the entire day reliving all of your good memories, sifting through the contents of your memory box (see chapter 3), and allowing yourself to face all of the pain you've been avoiding until now. You will cry out all of your tears until you have no more to shed.

You need to be absolutely alone for this experience, so plan for no interruptions. Disconnect the phone (or leave it off the hook), draw the curtains, muffle the doorbell (and put a DO NOT DISTURB sign on the door), and do not leave the house all day.

If you are truly frightened that you cannot bear all of the pain of a mourning day without doing something foolish, such as becoming suicidal, then arrange for a close friend to spend the day at your house. But that friend must go into another room from where you are and not "rescue" you except in a life-and-death emergency. If your grief is diluted, your day of mourning will have been wasted.

2. Eat sad foods. Plan to eat only those snacks or foods which will remind you of the person you loved—favorite foods or the same menu you served on one of those never-to-be-forgotten happy dates. Shop for and prepare the food the day before, if possible, so you won't have to interrupt your mourning to worry about what you are going to eat. Do not allow yourself to eat a large quantity of food or fun foods, because food can dull your pain and act as a pacifier.

During the day as you eat, take small bites and remember the last time you shared this food with your ex. Recapture the feeling of intimate sharing over a meal. The laughter. The shared jokes. What you talked about. Remind yourself that never again will you prepare or eat this food with that person. Allow yourself to experience the sadness of this thought. Cry if you feel like it.

3. *Arrange for sad smells.* Wear the cologne or perfume which was either a gift from or a favorite of the person who left you. If pine was a favorite scent, spray the room liberally with a pine air freshener. Burn incense, build a fire, barbeque hamburgers. Whatever smells or odors tend to remind you of that favorite person should be included in your mourning day experience.

Breathe in slowly, letting the smells trigger memories of your good times. That camping trip when you tramped through the pine trees. Sitting in front of the fireplace together, listening to the rain outside. Laughing at each other's efforts to get the barbeque fire to stay lit. Allow the pleasure of those memories to be ruined by the reality that the past is over. Experience your loss.

4. *Wear sad clothes.* You need to change clothes several times during the day to fully exorcise the ghosts from your closet. His favorite shirt. The bathing suit she bought you. The outfit you wore on your last date. Your wedding dress. Try to wear any clothes which may have any painful memories for at least part of the day.

Stand in front of a full-length mirror and look

at yourself in each outfit. Stroke the material; remember how you felt wearing that dress or shirt when you were with your beloved. If you have photos of the two of you when you were wearing that outfit, take them out and relive the day those pictures were taken. Smile again at the happy times. Imagine for a moment that they could return, then let go sadly, as you face the reality of being alone.

5. Listen to sad sounds. Play the music you used to share, especially "your song." Wind up the music box he gave you; turn a fan on the ceramic wind chimes she made for you. Lie down, close your eyes, and let the sounds surface hidden sadness from within your soul. Listen to the songs over and over until the sadness is replaced by weariness and maybe irritation at the repetitiveness of the sound.

6. Open the memory box. Retrieve the box from the garage or closet in which you have hidden all of your sad memorabilia and unpack one item at a time. Fondle each thing as you take it out of the box. Trace your beloved's face in the photograph with your finger. Try on the engagement ring. Open and smell the cologne. As you touch, smell and look at each object, itemize everything about it which reminds you of your lost love. Read old love letters and the "last love letter" you had started writing. Look at your wedding photos. Feel again the thrill of falling in love and the excitement of being loved in return. Seek to intensify your sadness with each item. Imagine that you are deliberately walking down the steps into a deep pit of sorrow. Only by facing the worst pain that each object can cause you—and surviving—will you rob that object of the power to ever hurt you again. Don't go on to the next object until you are totally bored by or indifferent to the first one.

And you will become bored! The body can only maintain an intense response to a particular stimulus for a limited period of time. Then the response is automatically adjusted. Diving into very cold water is a shock to the body, but within a short time the body adjusts to the change in temperature. People who live near airports or the freeway soon get used to the sounds of planes overhead or cars rushing by. Factory workers learn to tune out machine noise. Your eyes will adjust to the bright sunlight within minutes.

In a similar manner, when you have deliberately experienced the full force of sorrow triggered by a specific object, smell, sound or taste, and have allowed your physical, mental and emotional responses to run their courses, you will have adjusted to that stimulus. You have no more thoughts to explore, no more pain to feel, no more fear or sadness. It is boring.

When you are genuinely bored by a specific stimulus, continue touching, looking, listening or smelling it for a few more moments. Tell yourself several times, "I am bored by this _____ (name the object)." Speak aloud, using a firm, confident tone. Feel the exhilaration of conquering the ghosts in your life. You are alive; it is the past which is dead.

7. *Cleanse your heart.* Your heart probably feels worn out after all you have put it through today. Read Psalm 51 in which David prays for God to forgive his sin, to create a clean heart within him and to restore the joy of his salvation.

How could you paraphrase this psalm to:

A. Ask forgiveness for wrong attitudes or thoughts toward your ex?

B. Ask for God to take out the hurt which is wounding your soul? (Compare Psalm 51:7-11 with 1 John 1:7—2:3.)

C. Praise God in your own life?

Sometimes praising God is a sacrifice because your heart and spirit are broken. What do the following Scriptures say about this? Psalm 51:17; 107:22; 116:17; Jeremiah 33:11; 1 Thessalonians 5:18; Hebrews 13:15,16.

As you contemplate these verses, ask God to restore joy unto your heart as David did in Psalm 51:12.

8. Clean up the mess. By the end of your day of mourning, you will have made a giant mess of your home. The different clothes you have worn may be strewn around the room, the kitchen may be full of dirty dishes and leftover food. Your living room floor is probably cluttered with all of the objects from your memory box and the trash sack is overflowing with used tissues.

The mess is a good sign that you genuinely got into the spirit of mourning for the day. People who have taken the time to rehang all of the clothes, wash the dishes, and put away the records may not have given their full attention to grieving.

But now, the mess! Throw away anything which you don't want and that has no real value. Return to the box those things which you don't want or still evoke sad memories but which are valuable enough to give away to a charity. Keep things which are "historical" in nature from your relationship, for example, the photographs. Use those objects which you want to keep such as the radio, the tennis racket, the record albums. Valuable objects which you want to keep, but which are inappropriate for use just now (your engagement ring), can be put away or reclaimed (for example, by using the gold and diamonds from a wedding ring to make a dinner ring).

If you have some objects which belong to your ex and you think he/she might want them back, then put those aside for the next time you meet. You could mail or send these things to your ex with the children or through a friend. Don't use the returning of possessions as an excuse for contact with your ex at this point. If you are *insisting* on still remaining chummy "good friends" with your ex right now, perhaps you are fooling yourself about the reason you want to see that person. You may still be hooked on that relationship and haven't faced the fact that it is over.

9. Celebrate. Open the drapes, remove your DO NOT DISTURB sign, plug in the telephone and celebrate. You will have wanted to plan something special for the evening of your day of mourning. Do something you enjoy very much but don't often do. Be extravagant. Go out with a close friend. Or have a party. Buy the microwave oven you've been promising yourself. Or whatever will reward you for surviving a very scary experience; for being a conqueror!

Reclaiming Your World

Doug discovered that his world became very restricted within a few weeks after his girl friend Marilyn broke off with him. He couldn't go to all of their favorite restaurants or to the places they had visited together because the memories hurt too much. He avoided several streets and sections of town associated with Marilyn. He shopped only at a couple of stores where he was fairly certain that Marilyn would not be, and only during the hours she was at work. His choices of parties or recreational events were limited to those which would not be painful. In short, he avoided not only any possibility of accidental contact with Marilyn, but also any place which brought back memories of their relationship.

Temporary withdrawal is a great way to protect yourself while you rest, regroup and regain control of your life. But you cannot allow your world to be permanently restricted because the ghosts of your relationship live in all those special places. Doug, and you, must reclaim your worlds.

1. *List the haunted houses.* Identify all of the places you have been consciously, or subconsciously, avoiding because they remind you of your beloved. Don't forget your special bench by the lake at the park, the ice cream stand where he always bought you a butter brickle cone or she always ordered a double-dip combination of strawberry and chocolate ice cream. Think of places you have vacationed together or that you had planned to visit together. Any location which you fear might be painful for you to visit goes on the list.

2. *Exorcise the ghost.* Return (perhaps several times) to each of the places on your list and create new memories with which you will associate it in the future. *Desecrate* the place by going with someone else: a new friend of the opposite sex, a relative, a same sex friend, a noisy group of friends, or even a child. No longer will that table in

the restaurant or that box seat at the opera be *sacred* to the memories.

It's important to have fun on these return visits; don't go to experience the sadness or to mourn your loss. That is one reason you need to take someone with you rather than going alone. If you know someone who tends to make you feel less inhibited than usual, or who encourages you to laugh, act a little silly and just enjoy life—that's the person to ask to accompany you (at your expense, of course) on your crusade against the past.

Find new ways to enjoy yourself in these places you are visiting. If you always went to Aspen to ski, then go to eat dinner at the top of the mountain this time. If you always went to the park to sit by the water, feed the ducks and read poetry together, then go to play frisbee. If you and your ex used to enjoy eating at the marina, watching the sailboats at sea—then not only return to the marina, but also go out on one of the sailboats yourself.

The more times you return to a formerly *sacred* place with a new friend or many different people, and the more happy experiences you associate with that place, then the less you will feel saddened by the memories it once held for you. If your new experiences are bigger and better than the old memories, you will soon find that your world is expanding once again, and that you have been set free to explore that world.

People who allow their memories to restrict their worlds too long will discover that their fears become generalized. A woman whose happiest memories involved the years she and her husband lived in Hawaii can become afraid of not only returning to Hawaii, but also any island or even any place with a beach. A man whose girl friend had always accompanied him to concerts may not only be afraid of attending concerts in the civic auditorium, but may also avoid any type of musical event such as state fairs or church cantatas.

Linda and her husband had spent many a happy Saturday at the different swap meets around the country. After her divorce, Linda didn't just avoid the swap meets; she would go out of her way to not drive past a garage sale because of the sad feelings which would be triggered. Since garage sales seemed to be a neighborhood obsession that summer, she was hard pressed to avoid passing at least one every time she left the house. She decided that she had to take action to survive.

She called two friends, Richard and Amanda, and asked for their help. The three of them spent an entire day going from one garage sale to another—a grand total of twenty-six for the day! They sorted through paperback books, tried on old clothes, purchased a few odds and ends, and privately laughed at the crazy things some people were trying to sell.

Looking for more garage sales rather than avoiding them became Linda's goal for the day. And by eight o'clock that night she was tired, but cured of her irrational fear of swap meets and garage sales.

Pleasant Nostalgia

Once you've had your day of mourning and reclaimed your world by killing a few ghosts, you won't have lost all of your fond feelings for the past. Your painful memories will simply have mellowed into a pleasant nostalgia, much like you would feel if you returned to your old high school, or your room in the college dorm. You're still wistfully reminded of the past and the fun you once had, but things aren't the same anymore.

Affirmation of Joy

The joy of the Lord is in my heart. Repeat this affirmation several times a day. It is based on the following Scriptures:

Philippians 4:4—*Rejoice in the Lord always; again I will say, rejoice! (NASB).*

John 15:11—*These things I have spoken to you, that My joy may be in you, and that your joy may be made full (NASB).*

CHAPTER NINE

FACING THE FUTURE

"What can the future hold for me?" Marvin asks. "If my wife couldn't stand to live with me, or love me, I guess no one else could either."

Marvin is merely voicing the secret fears of many people who have been abandoned or rejected. People who are in long-term relationships tend to put all of their eggs in one basket, as it were, and when the basket is taken away the loss seems total and permanent. Because the one person you loved and trusted has violated that trust and rejected your love, you probably feel ugly and unlovable.

Perhaps a good look at yourself in the mirror or an honest self-appraisal only reinforces those feelings, because while you were taking care of your spouse, children or dating partner, you may have forgotten to take care of yourself! That's natural. The security of relationships can allow people to become comfortably self-neglecting.

You Are Beautiful and Lovable

With a little time, effort and attention you can be not only all you ever were, but more! Identify the areas of your life which need to be spruced up, enlivened or reawakened.

Does your body need attention? Remember how successfully you took charge of your spouse's diet? Or how you coached your son through football training? Give yourself the same attention. Develop an exercise plan you can live with and start shaping up. Join a gym, spa or health club. Asking a friend from work to join you in your exercise program will provide that extra incentive you may need to stick with the program. Go on a sensible diet. Set realistic weight loss goals and chart your progress.

Check out your wardrobe. When was the last time you bought yourself a really nice outfit? You may want to go to a fashion or color consultant for advice.

Change your hairstyle. Have your teeth capped. Learn how to apply the right makeup or to do your own nails with a professional flair.

Treat your body lovingly; not only is it your earthly house, it is also the temple of the Holy Spirit (see 1 Corinthians 6:19,20).

Some people discover that while involved in a long term relationship they have taken a break from personal and intellectual development. The college philosophy major hasn't cracked a book in years. The idealistic crusader of the sixties hasn't been taking the time to read the newspapers or listen to the news. Dust off some of those old interests and take a fresh look. You may discover that you would enjoy returning to college for a stimulating evening course, or getting involved in community action groups.

Reread your personal assets inventory and you will soon learn that you are not ugly or unlovable at all. You are a beautiful, exciting, stimulating and lovable person.

You Can Be Loved

Some people go through life always searching for love, yet never seem to find what they need. They go from one relationship to another, looking for that one partner who will be their all-in-all forever. The first problem with this approach is that no one human being can totally meet another's needs. There will be times when the needs of both persons will conflict and there will be disappointment.

The second basic problem with expecting just one person to meet your needs is that eventually the relationship will be over (by death, separation or divorce) and you will be left without the sole source of your love supply!

Jay is a good example. He was desperately unhappy following his divorce. He knew what he needed—a wife. Without a wife, he was convinced that he was condemned to a life of loneliness and lovelessness. Whenever he met a new woman, if there was any spark of mutual interest, he immediately thought, "Is this THE ONE for me?" His desperation communicated itself to the woman and she would usually withdraw.

Discussing this overwhelming loneliness with a friend, Jay explained his despair. "I need to be touched, held and loved. This was always the most beautiful part of making love with my wife. Now I can't have sex because God's Word says it is sin outside of marriage, so I must find another wife."

Later Jay came to recognize that he was making some false assumptions which were creating his deep, inner loneliness. By limiting affectionate touching to the experience of making love, Jay was ignoring all of the other sources of love and attention in his life. He learned that a friendly bear hug from friends of either sex made him feel loved and affirmed, and eased the ache of that inner loneliness. He became a "toucher," substituting hugs, an arm over the shoulder of a friend, brief, friendly kisses on the cheek, for handshakes or the wave of a hand in greeting. Jay's desperation eased because some of his needs for touching and being touched, for love and affection, were being met. His relationships with women improved.

If you, like Jay, have been thinking that you can be happy only by having one special person in your life, your response to being alone may be: deprivation, disillusionment, desperation or resignation. Emily Coleman and Betty Edwards explain these responses.[1]

1. Deprivation. You have found the one person whom you believe can provide you with all of the love you need or want. So you avoid all other relationships, gestures of friendship, love and attention. You hone in on your one source until it dries up and leaves you starving.

2. Disillusionment. You develop a relationship with someone you believe can meet your needs, but later discover that only some of your needs and wants are being met. So you break off the relationship and start looking for the one person who can be all you expect in a partner.

3. Desperation. You are driven by a sense of urgency to find the mate of your dreams, and are constantly searching. Your approach tends to be a little too eager, too aggressive and too overwhelming. In your search for your one true love, you overlook a lot of friendships which could enrich your life.

4. Resignation. Past relationships have failed, your search for a perfect mate has been futile and you are resigned to the idea that you will never again be loved. You become bitter, resentful of the happiness of others, and withdraw into a protective shell to avoid future disappointments.

These approaches are all nonproductive! You are not doomed to a life without love. You can have a supportive network of caring friends who will help you fulfill your needs and desires for love, affirmation, affection and attention.

Your Thoughts Control Your Fears

You are probably a little frightened of facing life alone or of the possibility that you will never have another love relationship. These fears about future possibilities, however, are expressed in your thoughts as actual statements of fact and are played and replayed inside your mind until you begin to believe them.

Maybe your response to rejection is to think, "I will never be loved again." Or, "I cannot have a permanent relationship." Or, "I am ugly." As you begin to believe these statements, you act on them. You don't go to a party *because you are ugly.* You won't go out on a date with a new man or woman *because you'll never be loved again.* Or you won't make new friends *because you can-*

not have a permanent relationship. You develop phobias toward parties, dates, friends and meeting people.

The solution is to discover the negative statements with which you are torturing yourself and replace them with positive affirmations. Just as you have acted in a certain negative way because of fear-based, negative (and false) thoughts, so you will notice that when you reprogram your mind with positive, realistic affirmations, your behaviors will become positive.

If you think that you are shy and afraid of meeting people, then you will probably not look a stranger in the eyes, initiate conversations at social gatherings, or go to very many parties. If, on the other hand, you believe that you are outgoing and love meeting people, then you will probably approach and talk self-confidently with people in any setting. Your actions are the results of your thoughts about yourself.

At first you may have difficulty behaving the way a self-confident, assertive, loving, friendly or brave person would. If so, then ask yourself, "How would I act if I were that way?" Then do so! Soon the new behavior pattern will become more familiar and comfortable and you will see people responding to you as if you were the person you wish you were! That's because by then you will be! You will have changed your behavior by changing your thoughts!

Interestingly, you will also influence how other people relate to you because you are giving them a new and positive message. Terrie used to tell herself that no one would find her interesting or want to talk to her. Because she believed herself to be boring, she didn't exert herself during conversations or try to be entertaining. Consequently, few people went out of their way to talk with Terrie, which reinforced her self-concept of being dull and boring.

When Terrie discarded her negative self statements and replaced them with positive affirmations, her behavior changed. She told herself, "I am an interesting conversationalist and people find me fascinating." Then she began to behave as if she were interesting, fluent and fascinating. She worked at improving her communicating skills, and people responded with interest. Today, Terrie is usually at the center of the group of people at a party or social event who appear to be having the most fun.

You too can change the way people respond to you. Replace your negative attitudes with positive affirmations.

Instead of saying, "I am not lovable," say, "I am a very lovable person." Think of the things which make you such a lovable person—the way you care about others, your generosity, your honesty. Focus on those characteristics and develop other similar qualities. Soon you will think of yourself as being more lovable, and so will others. Their response will reinforce your new attitude and you will become even more lovable!

Don't get the idea that your negative attitudes are silly; they started as observations of or responses to past bad experiences. If you touched a stove and suffered a severe burn, your mental response would probably be, "If I touch a stove, I will get burned." However, you don't avoid stoves altogether for the rest of your life! Instead, you become cautious about touching stoves, learning to check whether or not the surface is hot. You change your mental response to "If I touch a *HOT* stove, I will get burned." And you learn to discriminate between hot stoves and safe ones. In much the same way you will want to identify erroneous responses to bad experiences in relationships, and to discriminate between a real and an imagined outcome of risking again.

Ensure your recovery by developing a positive outlook and reprogramming your attitudes and actions. Most likely you will meet someone who will love and care for you. If you really were ugly or unlovable, then you would not have already had a special relationship. The fact that someone has loved and cared for you in the past proves that you are beautiful and lovable. Believe it!

Recapture Your *Joie de Vivre*

Can you remember being a child who was unafraid of anything? Who could never refuse a dare? Who could approach new situations with an enthusiastic energy? Have you lost some of your spontaneous excitement? Learn to recapture your sense of adventure.

Get away by yourself and spend an hour or two reliving your memories of that carefree period. (It may help to close your eyes and go through a few relaxation exercises first.) Picture yourself as vividly as possible. See yourself in a favorite outfit. Remember the smells, the colors, the other people who were a part of your world at that time. Stop the memory newsreel and relive in minute detail certain special experiences. Can you remember exactly who said what and how you felt and what you were thinking, but didn't say?

When you are ready to stop daydreaming, ask yourself (and answer) several questions about the child you used to be. For example:

1. What did you most enjoy doing?

2. What used to make you happy? laugh? excited?

3. What roles did you assume at home? In your peer groups? With members of the opposite sex?

4. Which roles were most comfortable? enjoyable? fun? mischievous?

5. How did you try to gain love, attention and respect?

6. Which methods were most successful?

7. What daydreams, fantasies or goals did you have?

8. Who were your heroes? Why?

9. Who exerted the most influence in your life at that time?

10. What kind of self-image did you have? How was it reinforced?

The next step is to update those past observations into present possibilities. Consider how you answered the above questions as you *write your answers* to the next ten.

1. What things that you used to enjoy doing, but haven't done lately, can you do *now*?

2. How can you recreate some past, pleasant experiences today, tomorrow or this week?

3. What roles, which you used to enjoy, can you assume again—perhaps temporarily, or just for fun? (i.e., teacher, leader, follower, nurturer, adventurer)

4. Which positive, successful ways to gain love, attention or respect can you repeat now?

5. Which of your childhood daydreams, goals or fantasies could you make come true right now?

6. Which of those goals or dreams could you fulfill if you worked at it hard and long enough?

7. In what ways have you copied your childhood heroes?

8. Is there any way to contact someone who used to be your hero?

9. Have your heroes changed? How and why?

10. What things did you always want to do as a child, but were not able (or allowed) to do, but you could try now?

Keep your written answers and find ways to recapture your *joie de vivre* by repeating, updating or reassuming activities, childhood dreams or roles.

Barbara, a boisterous tomboy at ten, but a quiet lady at thirty, found excitement in taking an aerobics exercise class and in learning to sail.

Stuart had always wanted to live dangerously as a boy (climbing the highest trees, walking the river bridge railing, and jumping his bicycle off ramps); but as an adult he had focused on building security for himself and his family. After his divorce he rediscovered his old enthusiasm for the thrill of danger. He took up hang gliding and became an entertaining enthusiast of the sport.

Try to enrich your life by reviving your old interests.

—Were you a budding actress? Get involved in a community theater group or a drama class.

—Were you a writer? Set up a writing corner in your home and start creating.

—Did you ever enjoy painting or drawing? Try it again.

You don't have to be a professional or an expert; just enjoy yourself. And because you'll be having so much fun, you will become a more interesting person to know.

Revamp Your Expectations

You may be afraid of the future and miserable in the present because your expectations are unrealistic and obsolete. If your expectation is that everyone will fall in love with you, or that you can only be happy as long as there is someone who is in love with you, you will probably be disappointed.

Dawn thought that being loved in a romantic way by a husband was the only thing she wanted in life. When her husband left her, she assumed she could not be satisfied until she remarried. Several relationships later, Dawn decided that romance did not meet her deep, inner needs. She reflected that even in her marriage she had not felt totally accepted as a person of worth.

As she developed a network of supportive friendships, Dawn discovered that loving acceptance was far more fulfilling than just romance! She felt stronger then ever before and concentrated on building solid friendships. A year later she did remarry—one of the men who had become a close friend before a romance between them developed.

You may find that planning to date again is very frightening because you see it as reentering the rat race to "find someone" rather than as a way to share fun activities and experiences with a member of the opposite sex. Dating is a process, not a project to catch someone. Rather than waiting for and expecting to find one person who is willing to spend the rest of his/her life with you, look for someone who wants to spend an hour or an evening together. "Forever" commitments are difficult to find; but there are a lot of people who will commit to sharing an evening.

By evaluating your expectations, you can discard those which are no longer appropriate, revise a few, and develop a set of realistic hopes which are likely to be fulfilled.

Risking Reaching Out

If you have followed the suggestions in this chapter you have found that your fears of the future are manageable, and that you have a lot to look forward to. You are lovable and can be loved. By trading in your negative attitudes for positive affirmations, recapturing your earlier zest for living, and revising your expectations, you have taken charge of your life and are ready to risk reaching out.

Affirmation of Emotional Control

The Holy Spirit controls my emotions. I am gentle, kind, loving and affirming. Repeat this affirmation several times a day. It is based on the following Scriptures:

Ephesians 4:29a—*Do not let any unwholesome talk come out of your mouths, but only what is helpful for building others up according to their needs (NIV).*

Colossians 3:12-14—*Therefore, as God's chosen people, holy and dearly loved, clothe yourselves with compassion, kindness, humility, gentleness and patience. Bear with each other and forgive whatever grievances you may have against one another. Forgive as the Lord forgave you. And over all these virtues put on love, which binds them all together in perfect unity (NIV).*

Note
1. Emily Coleman and Betty Edwards, *Brief Encounters* (Garden City, NY: Doubleday and Co., Inc., 1979).

CHAPTER TEN
BUILDING FRIENDSHIPS

You're all geared up to reach out and build new or restructure old friendships. Now what? Where do you start?

Let People Know You're Available

Consider the people in your classes, church, organizations or where you work. Are there some you would like to get to know better? Ask them out for a cup of coffee/tea, one at a time and get acquainted.

Ask your co-workers about interesting things to do on weekends; express a desire to be invited on one of their water ski excursions or to the office softball game.

Call your friends and let them know you are ready to get involved again in life and would like to meet new and exciting people (of both sexes). Tell them you've just been through a difficult time and need their help in getting back into circulation. (You don't need to go into the details of your breakup or divorce; just mention that you are single or unattached again.)

Review Your Current Friendships
Most of us need three types of friendships: intimate, close and casual.

1. Intimate friends are those *four to seven* people whose emotional support of and depth of involvement with you are strong. These friends:
—are readily available to you
—understand, like and accept you as you are and where you are in your personal and spiritual development
—are dependable
—have very frequent contact with you.

Intimate friends provide you with emotional support.

2. Close friends are those *fifteen to twenty* people who are important in your life, whom you see fairly regularly. These friends:
—make a conscious choice to spend time with you
—provide companionship.

They provide enrichment in your life.

3. Casual friends are those *thirty to fifty* people who have some intermittent contact with you, but who are not what you would consider close friends. These people:
—are in contact only infrequently, and then usually for a specific reason (holiday) or activity (golfing)
—are often resources (get you tickets, help you improve your golf game, provide information about a job)

Casual friends tend to provide stimulation in

your life (physical, intellectual, or cultural).

Each of these types of friends is important in your life. You will want members of both sexes, singles and marrieds, young and not so young people in each of your friendship circles. Each friendship will require your attention and nourishment to be maintained. But friendships are not static; they are dynamic, always changing.

People move from one level of friendship to another as the priorities in their lives fluctuate. People will weave in and out of your life as circumstances change. This movement has both advantages and disadvantages we must appreciate and accept. You will want to prepare yourself to cope with such changes by learning to risk reaching out and building good friendships quickly. But most of all, by learning to enjoy, treasure and let go of short-term friendships.

Assess your friendships to determine if your supportive network is a solid structure. First, identify your friends by listing their names on a sheet of paper under one of the following categories: intimate, close, casual. Then evaluate your social structure by answering the following questions:

1. Do you have enough—but not too many—names under each category?

2. Have you listed all of the names as casual friends and none as intimate? Or vice versa?

3. Do you have a balance of same sex and opposite sex friends? Singles and marrieds?

4. Do the people you have listed as intimate friends provide the emotional support you need?

5. Do your close friends enrich your life?

6. Do your casual friends stimulate and add

excitement to your life-style?

If your supportive network seems deficient in some of these areas, then set some goals and start building the types of friendships you need.

Remodel Your Support System

Here are several ideas for updating and strengthening your friendship support system.

1. Let go of nonproductive relationships. Are you investing a significant amount of energy in trying to maintain one-sided friendships? Do you continue to write long, personal letters to high school friends who rarely, if ever, write back? Perhaps that investment might be better spent on improving other friendships or developing new ones.

Maybe instead of completely letting go of some friendships, you might simply keep them as casual relationships rather than intimate or close ones.

2. Improve existing relationships. Make room in your intimate or close friendship circles for one or two additional friends. Select a close friend you'd like to become an intimate, or a casual friend who could become close.

Share your desires to develop a deeper relationship with that person. If he/she is willing, then seek to spend additional time alone together sharing, working together on a project, or doing activities of interest to both of you.

Another way to develop improved relationships is to break out of the roles you have fallen into with one another. If you are always the listener when Sally comes over, then agree that next time you will be the one to talk most. If you are the one who is always organized, taking charge and taking care of everyone else, let the others experience that role and take care of you for a change.

3. *Add new people to your social structure.* Go to interesting places, get involved in fun activities and always be ready and open to starting conversations. Carry a copy of a book that makes a statement about who you are or what interests you. Use the book to initiate conversations. Look for things to discuss with strangers. For example:

—to someone carrying an interesting book: "How do you like that book?" Or, "Do you agree with the author's viewpoint?"

—to a person standing in line near you at a theater: "What have you heard about this play?" Or, "What made you decide to see this play?"

—to someone wearing an unusual belt, hat, suit, coat, or carrying a unique purse or briefcase: "Where did you ever find that fascinating belt (or coat, purse, briefcase)?" Or, "Did you have that belt (purse, briefcase) made especially for you?"

If an interesting conversation develops you might decide to have a cup of coffee/tea or lunch together and get acquainted.

Develop Relational Skills

If you have had problems in the past with developing and maintaining friendships, perhaps you need to develop the skills for doing so.

1. *Use small talk.* Initiating conversations with strangers usually involves small talk, getting their attention without scaring them away. People have a zone of privacy, a psychological space, which must be entered if you are to reach them. But barging into that space too quickly results in

their feeling invaded and your being rebuffed. So curb your natural impatience and learn the art of discussing the inconsequential.

2. Take risks. Be willing to be the one who reaches out first to start conversations, or be vulnerable in order to put the other person at ease. Share a little of yourself when asking about the other. For example, in a hospital waiting room you might say, "I'm very worried; my grandfather is having difficult surgery just now. Why are you here?"

Or at a social gathering, "I'm new in town and a little nervous about coming to a party such as this where I don't know anyone. How about you?"

3. Keep conversations going. Sometimes you have to work extra hard to keep a conversation from dying when the other person is not very communicative. In those cases, be sure not to ask questions which can be answered with one or two words. *Not,* "Do you like living in this town?" *But,* "What do you like about living here?"

Also, learn to pick up on hidden clues in the other's remarks which you can pursue as conversational topics.

4. Listen. Take time to listen when people talk with you. Try to hear as much of what they are not saying as of what they are.

Remember important things like names, the fact that a new grandchild has been born, or a new car purchased. When a new friend remembers that you drink your coffee black instead of offering you cream and sugar each time, you feel that he/she cares enough to listen to what you say.

Listen with an open mind as others express their personal feelings or opinions. You don't have to always argue your point. Allow others to disagree with you.

5. Care. Get involved with people on a caring level. Learn what problems they're facing, what dreams they're striving for. Take time to make that congratulatory phone call or to mail a card saying you care and are praying for them.

Show you care by your actions. Be available to help when needed.

6. Be real. Allow your friends to see the real you. The person who isn't always right, confident, unafraid or happy. Share your joys and your disappointments, your hopes and fears. If your friends believe that you have your life totally together and don't need any help, they will probably not provide the emotional support you do need.

Instead of expecting people to read your mind and anticipate your needs, ask for what you want. For example, tell a friend you are feeling low and wish he/she would come over and spend a couple of hours cheering you up.

Dr. Debora Phillips suggests practicing being assertive in the following ways:[1]

Accepting compliments. Practice accepting compliments for a couple of weeks by acknowledging them rather than rejecting them.

Expressing opinions. At least twice a day express an opinion to someone. Start with the easy ones. "I think we should go out to lunch today." Then work up to those which are more difficult for you to express.

Saying "I." At least five times a day start a sentence with I. Instead of saying, "The building is cold!" Say, "I am cold!"

Sensing feelings. Stop several times a day (at

least eight) and scan your feelings to identify what you are experiencing at that moment.

Expressing feelings. A few times a day (at least two as appropriate) express what you are feeling to someone else.

Modeling. Whenever you need extra confidence, imagine how a confident person would act in the situation you are in and copy the behaviors you imagine. Think of and use a confident tone, words and gestures.

Saying no. If saying no is not easy for you, then practice saying no at least twice a week when someone asks you to do something which will not be convenient for you to do. (This is not saying that you should be unkind, just more assertive about how your time may be imposed upon if you aren't honest with others.)

Asking favors. If you rarely ask favors, then try asking a friend to do something with or for you at least once a week. Start with simple, easy favors such as having coffee/tea together.

As you make it easier for people to relate to you and to get close enough to become friends, you will find that you are gaining new friends all of the time. Your support structure will soon be strong.

Affirmation of a Positive Self-Image
I am the unique person God designed me to be. I like His design. Repeat this affirmation several times a day. It is based on the following Scriptures:

Psalm 139:13,14a—*For Thou didst form my inward parts; Thou didst weave me in my mother's womb. I will give thanks to Thee, for I am fearfully and wonderfully made (NASB).*

Ephesians 2:10—*For we are God's workman-
ship, created in Christ Jesus to do good works,
which God prepared in advance for us to do
(NIV).*

Note
1. Debora Phillips, *How to Fall Out of Love* (New York: Faw-
cett Book Group, 1978).

CHAPTER ELEVEN

FALLING IN LOVE AGAIN

When there is a lack of a *significant other*, even the best supportive network of friends seems inadequate at times. Separate from the general loneliness of being newly uncoupled is a specific longing to love and be loved by a person of the opposite sex. So you have probably started (or been thinking of starting) to date again.

I'm Scared

Perhaps the very idea of falling in love or choosing a commitment frightens you. Take a close look at your fears. Can you identify with any of the following examples?

1. Fear of rejection. Darlene is so afraid of rejection that she actually rejects others before they can turn away first.

Conrad's conversations are laced with frequent self-criticism in an attempt to prevent others from criticizing him. He equates criticism with rejection.

Sheryl virtually withdrew from the world, her friends and all men so she would never risk being rejected again.

Thor holds friendships at arm's length, figuring that if people don't get too close, they can't hurt him.

Charlene does much the opposite. She rushes to an intimate level as quickly as possible, relating her life story, secret dreams and private disappointments almost at first meeting. Like a person who closes the eyes and dives into an unfamiliar river, she often finds the waters filled with painful surprises.

2. Fear of a bad relationship. As soon as Molly recovered from the initial pain of being rejected by her ex-husband, she admitted that the relationship hadn't been all that good. She vowed that never again would she allow herself to be stuck in a bad relationship. The problem now is that at the first hint of disharmony in a new dating relationship, Molly breaks off the association. She may soon run out of men to date, since disagreements arise in any friendship.

Don's approach is similar to Molly's, but a bit more organized. On the first date he quizzes the woman to determine their compatibility. If too many differences or problems surface, then there is no second date. While the principle involved may not be bad, the fact that Don has a written list of fifty-seven items to discuss and frequently refers to the list during the conversation is somewhat disconcerting to his dates!

One reason people are afraid of being rejected or of being stuck in a bad relationship is because they haven't worked through the problems of the last relationship. This is a mistake.

What Went Wrong?

When people go from one relationship to another without assessing what went wrong, they are likely to find that the same problems exist in most of their relationships. Take an hour or two to analyze prior relationships and identify possible patterns of behavior which contributed to the eventual termination of the relationship. Some areas to consider include:

1. Conflict resolution. Whenever there was a difference in what you wanted to do (or buy, or eat), how was that difference resolved? Did you simply do neither and agree on a third selection instead? Or did the same person always give in? Did that person then pout or make demands to compensate for having given in? Or did the person who usually gave in stop expressing personal preferences and just let the other person make all of the decisions? Were some problems never resolved, and became sources of frequent clashes?

In a healthy partnership, there is mutual respect for each person's needs, desires, and preferences, and an honest attempt to resolve problems/differences so that both persons win.

So, in your new relationships, share what you like and dislike, decide what you are willing to give and what you want from the other, and develop a problem-solving approach which will work for the two of you.

2. Communication. Did both of you feel free to discuss all of your feelings with each other? Was the trust level high enough so that you could share those feelings or your ideas or dreams, without fear of being belittled, ridiculed, rejected or ignored?

When you talked, did both of you really listen to what was being said?

The depth of a relationship is both reflected in and a function of the level of communication between the two people involved.

So, in your new relationship, care enough to be open, risk vulnerability and even confront lovingly as the need arises.

3. Acceptance and affirmation. Were both of you accepted by the other for whom—and what—you were? Or did one of you have hopes of changing the other into a "more acceptable person"? (Tess secretly hoped her boyfriend, who was a salesperson, would soon become the store manager. But he was happy as a salesperson and didn't want to become a manager!)

Did one of you tend to criticize or nag the other? Both privately or in public?

Did one of you frequently ask the other, "Do you love me?"

Were compliments, affectionate touching, or other affirmations infrequent? Did one person tend to forget birthdays, anniversaries or other special days? Was one of you habitually late for your dates?

A strong love relationship will usually include mutual acceptance and affirmation. Both persons will feel loved and accepted—because they are!

So, in future relationships, take time to affirm your partner and to let your love show. Allow the other person to be, and don't try to make changes!

4. Activities. Did you spend a significant

amount of your time (outside of working hours) away from each other, doing things with other people, or alone?

Was most of the time you were together spent at parties, movies or generally with other people?

Were you primarily involved in together activities which did not involve talking, sharing or helping each other?

A relationship develops and grows when people spend time alone together, talking, sharing, creating things, or working on projects which require interaction.

So take time to plan and follow through on those kinds of projects, and to spend more quality time alone together.

Relationships do not fall apart overnight. If you are observant enough you can usually spot early warning signs of deterioration. By reflecting on what went wrong in prior relationships, you will be better prepared to prevent those same problems from breaking up a future relationship.

New Ways of Relating

If you have discovered patterns of behaviors which were nonproductive in prior relationships, you will want to learn ways of changing those ways of relating.

Chester grew up in a home where little affection was shown unless a family member was ill. Illness was also the only excuse for not completing assigned tasks. Chester learned early in life that being sick was the easy way to get the love and attention he needed. So whenever he was under pressure, felt insecure or needed extra love, he developed a slight fever, a cold or a headache. (Our bodies are very cooperative this way. If you think you need to be sick, you will be!)

Chester didn't unlearn this method of coping with stress or insecurity, so as an adult he was often ill. The problem was that his wife hated illness, so whenever Chester became ill, she gave him less loving attention. This made him feel less loved, more insecure and consequently more sick!

Chester must learn a better way of getting the love and attention he needs.

Kimberly's problem is different. She is so lonely and hates being alone so much that it doesn't matter what the new person does, as long as he is there! The problem is that eventually that person does one irritating thing too many, or does the one thing Kimberly cannot tolerate, and she blows up and walks away. Usually she feels taken advantage of because she had "overlooked so much" during the relationship.

For example, Kimberly dated Frank for several months. She let him (by saying nothing) bring his laundry for her to do during their "at-home" dates. She encouraged (by not objecting) him to tear down and work on his car in her driveway for weeks. By not mentioning the issue, she allowed Frank to make several long-distance calls on her telephone without paying her for them. When Frank came in one day and asked her to mend several pants and sew buttons on a few shirts, Kimberly threw the clothes in his face!

And as far as Frank was concerned he had simply taken one more liberty. Kimberly considered it *one too many*!

But by not saying anything about those things

which were bothering her all along for fear of upsetting the relationship, Kimberly had been giving silent permission for those behaviors to continue.

Kimberly must learn to be assertive, not passive or aggressive, in relationships if she is ever to have a successful long-term association.

Miriam has a habit of not being herself in a man-woman friendship. When she and Dennis first started dating, she always let him choose what they would do and where they would go. Just *being* with Dennis felt so good that she didn't care if they were doing things she wouldn't have enjoyed by herself. So she spent Sunday afternoons watching sports on television, Tuesdays eating Chinese food, and Saturdays playing golf. Because Dennis was so sure of himself, Miriam rarely voiced an idea. She wore her hair to please him and dressed to his taste. When she was hurt by Dennis's thoughtlessness or public criticism, Miriam waited until she was alone to cry. She was afraid that if she were to say anything, Dennis might reject her and she didn't want to lose him.

At first Dennis felt that he had found the perfect mate—a woman who liked all of the same things he did! But after several months, Dennis began to feel that Miriam was not adding anything to the relationship. She was more a passenger than a partner! Finally, he encouraged her to be more assertive than she had been.

When Miriam took Dennis at his word and started expressing preferences, ideas and opinions, Dennis discovered that the two of them had little in common! Surprised, he broke off the relationship.

Miriam was hurt. And angry! Yet she had set herself up for hurt because she had not been real with Dennis. She had led Dennis to believe that she was the person she had pretended to be! If someone likes you because of the false image you project, it is the image they like, not the real you!

Miriam needs to learn to be real in relating in order to have a genuine relationship.

Luke tends to have only one close friend at a time—the woman he is dating. This results in his being quite jealous of any time she spends with any of her other friends or family members. He becomes possessive, insecure, and demanding.

Luke needs a better support system—several close friends—in order not to cling so tightly to a dating partner as to virtually smother the relationship.

Whatever patterns of problem behavior you may have discovered you want to discard, you will find that changing those patterns will take work! The new behaviors will not be comfortable at first. You may want to rehearse them before actually trying them. Imagine a situation in which you might need to use the new behavior, and decide just what you will say and do. Develop several plot variations for the incident so you can decide on different ways to implement the new relational style.

Practice saying aloud certain sentences you might use so that you get used to hearing yourself making those statements or asking those questions.

It might help if you asked a friend to roleplay the situation with you several times so that you will feel more comfortable with the new behaviors.

Walk—Don't Run

Don't rush into a new love too quickly! Continuing the analogy of addiction, Dr. Wanderer reminds us that most of our society is addicted to love and is out looking for a connection. Little doses of love are easily found, but the big score, a committed, long-term relationship, isn't that easy to find.

And much like an addict without a connection who settles for any drug from any dealer (sometimes settling for "bad stuff") a person desperate for love may settle for a "bad" relationship rather than be without love.

And, because that person is no longer lonely, and has stopped hurting, it is assumed that *this is real love*! Lack of pain is not love!

So go out, make friends, date, care—but wait a while before declaring that you are in love again. If you have, indeed, found a new love relationship, it will last long enough for you to be sure. Meanwhile, work together to build a foundation of solid friendship for your new love relationship.

Ask God to guide you and your new partner as you build your relationship. Ask for wisdom and insight. Spend time with God and in the Word shoring up your spiritual life. Focus on becoming the person God planned for you to be.

Affirmation of Love

I am a loving, giving, genuine person. Repeat this affirmation several times a day. It is based on the following Scriptures:

John 13:34,35—*A new commandment I give you: Love one another. As I have loved you, so you must love one another. All men will know that you are my disciples if you love one another (NIV).*

1 John 4:7—*Dear friends, let us love one another, for love comes from God. Everyone who loves has been born of God and knows God (NIV).*

CHAPTER TWELVE

STAYING FRIENDS WITH YOUR EX

At some point, after working through all of the different responses of being rejected which have been discussed in this book, you will discover a marvelous feeling of freedom. Your mourning process is over.

—Your thinking is sharper and clearer.

—Your decisions are more reliable.

—Your concentration is better.

—Your feelings are more alive.

You have recovered your dignity, self-esteem, perspective, balance, security, control and a sense of being lovable and valuable. Your spiritual life has improved, and you are daily affirming strength, faith, growth, thought-control, having your needs met, peace, forgiveness, joy, emotional control, a positive self-image, love (and this week, adding achievement) in your life.

You have let go of the past, started living in the now, and are facing the future unafraid.

When you reach this place you have one unfinished task to accomplish—reconnecting with your ex and reestablishing the friendship. Your *recovery* is over. Time for *rediscovery*!

Am I Ready?

If the thought of seeing your ex again causes you to either panic or palpitate, then you are probably not quite ready. There are several reasons you will want to one day reopen the lines of communication with your ex if possible:

—You might still live in the same area and continuing to try and avoid one another will be bothersome.

—If there are children involved, it is best if both parents can relate to each other with respect and courtesy.

—A permanent division between two members of the Body of Christ can be a hindrance in their lives to the work of the Holy Spirit.

—Until there is a right relationship between both parties, the full work of forgiveness has not been effected, according to David Augsburger.[1]

—You had a (possibly long-term) relationship with your ex, which usually means that you counted that person as your best friend. It doesn't make a lot of sense to toss that friendship away just because you are no longer a couple.

You will know that you are ready to meet with your ex when you can look forward to that meeting with the same pleasure that you would if you were seeing any other old friend. If you have a sense of panic, you may need to reread and follow the behavioral suggestions in some of the first eleven chapters of this book. Also, if your anticipation causes you to start fantasizing again, you can be fairly certain that you are still hung up on your ex.

Planning to Meet

Plan to get together for breakfast or lunch (not dinner, this is not a date) because the meal itself will give you something to do to bridge any awkward moments. Also, the restaurant should be a neutral location—not one you can associate with past memories when you and your ex had a love relationship.

Set a time limit for the meeting. Two hours is more than sufficient for this first time.

Don't dress to impress your ex with how much sexier, attractive, thinner or desirable you are now than you were before. On the other hand, don't show up in your sloppy, gardening togs! Just wear what you would if you were seeing an old friend—which is what you are doing.

Consider what you will talk about. No arguing about support checks, visitation issues, or divorce settlements. No recriminations, nasty digs, or tender reminiscing. No rehashing old quarrels.

Instead, ask about how the job is going and share about your own. Discuss the children. Ask about accomplishments and share what new things you're trying.

The only people at this meeting should be you and your ex. Neither of you should bring along anyone else. This is between the two of you and other people would only add to the stress—the person who would be a support for you might appear as a threat to your ex, and vice versa.

If you are now dating someone new, tell that person of your plans to meet your ex to reopen communications. Be sensitive that your new partner may be threatened by your plan and may need additional affirmation from you to keep from fantasizing about you and your ex walking off into the sunset together! Spend time with your new partner before going to see your ex—and perhaps afterwards also.

Before you contact your ex about getting together you will want to prepare your heart by having a long quiet time with God. Ask Him to calm your emotions and give you wisdom.

When you have decided you are ready and have considered where you would like to take your ex for breakfast or lunch (your treat, of course), call your ex and arrange to meet. Remember that the other person may not be ready to see you again and your getting together may have to be postponed for a while.

Lingering Doubts

In the back of your mind you may have a few lingering doubts about your ability to handle the meeting. You may wonder if you will burst into tears, become angry or have some other inappropriate response. If those doubts turn into fears which start to seriously bother you, then prepare for the meeting in the following ways.

1. Fantasize as vividly as possible about the meeting, mentally rehearsing how you will behave and what you will say.

2. Go to the restaurant and eat the same meal as you plan to share with your ex. Imagine your ex sitting across the table from you while you eat. Think of what you will be saying to that person during the meal.

3. Take a friend with you—your new dating

partner, for example—and have a pleasant meal together. (Then if the meeting with your ex isn't going as well as you had hoped, you can flash back to the last time you were there with another friend, under more pleasant circumstances!)

The Meeting

Allow plenty of time to arrive at the restaurant early enough to not feel rushed. When your ex arrives, smile your brightest and greet him/her warmly. Shake hands, hug briefly or give a light kiss on the cheek. Exchange pleasantries to get through any possible awkwardness. Be understanding if your ex is not sure of how to cope with the meeting. Remember, this is a new, unfamiliar role for both of you. You are probably more prepared than your ex because you've been working through this book!

If you find yourself getting weepy during the meeting, don't overreact. It's OK to express honest emotions. On the other hand, if you become overwhelmed with a desire to bawl your eyes out, you may want to excuse yourself and go to the restroom for a few minutes. If you cannot regain your composure, you could send a note to your ex saying that something has come up and you had to leave but that you'll call later. *Note:* Don't forget to pay the check on your way out!

It's quite possible that you will find yourself getting turned on sexually at the sight of your ex. After all, you were attracted to that person in the first place. Don't take your feelings too seriously; and if your ex suddenly turns amorous, just ignore it or treat it lightly. The purpose of this meeting is not to get you hooked again on your ex.

When the time you have set for the meeting is up, bring the conversation to an end, and leave. Agree to keep in touch and to get together again soon.

How Friendly to Be

Each ex-couple will have to decide what works best for them. But there are some guidelines to keep in mind.

1. Don't start rebuilding a dependency relationship with your ex. You have been taking good care of yourself for several weeks now, and doing fine. You don't want to undo all of your work!

2. Don't get into a financial relationship with your ex. Going into business together, lending or borrowing money is probably just asking for trouble later on.

3. Stay out of the clinches. Avoid evening encounters which could turn into pseudo dates—particularly if neither of you is dating anyone else at this time. You might slip back into the familiar romantic roles and start the rejection cycle all over again.

4. Share. Do some safe activities together, such as those you would feel comfortable doing with an old friend or a friend of the same sex.

5. Explore and learn your new roles. You will want to avoid slipping back into your old roles—either romantic or angry. You will probably not become "best friends" for a long time, if ever.

Forgiven and Free to Be

When you and your ex come through the rejection experience to a friendship relationship, you will find that the mutual forgiveness which occurs sets you both free to grow and build a future separate from each other.

Remember that even if you were not the person who walked out of the relationship, the problems which led to the breakup were shared by the two of you. There is almost never only one person at fault when a relationship comes apart. Both people lose in rejection, not just the person who is "abandoned." So, even though you may feel you were the only one who was wronged, your ex probably has some hurt also. Care enough to reach out first to reestablish your friendship.

Actually, until the pain of the past has been worked through and let *go of*, neither of you is really ready to build new, healthy relationships with other people.

So, say with Paul:

I haven't got it all together yet. But I have learned to forget and let go of the pain of past relationships and to stretch forth to new relationships which are ahead, to discover and achieve what God has waiting for me (Philippians 3:13,14, paraphrased to fit the context.)

Then go out. LIVE!

. . . AND LOVE AGAIN!

Affirmation of Achievement

I am a growing person who sets and achieves godly goals. Repeat this affirmation several times a day. It is based on the following Scriptures:

Philippians 3:13,14—*Brothers, I do not consider myself yet to have taken hold of it. But one thing I do: Forgetting what is behind and straining toward what is ahead, I press on toward the goal to win the prize for which God has called me heavenward in Christ Jesus (NIV).*

Titus 3:8—*This is a trustworthy saying. And I want you to stress these things, so that those who have trusted in God may be careful to devote themselves to doing what is good. These things are excellent and profitable for everyone (NIV).*

Note
1. David Augsburger, *Caring Enough to Forgive* (Ventura, CA: Regal Books, 1981).

Other Regal Books to help you build better relationships